the Joy of Baking

THE EVERYDAY ZEN OF WATCHING BREAD RISE

Steph Blackwell

greenfinch

First published in Great Britain in 2021 by
Greenfinch
An imprint of Quercus Editions Ltd
Carmelite House
50 Victoria Embankment
London EC4Y 0DZ

An Hachette UK company

A CIP catalogue record for this book is available
from the British Library

HB ISBN 978-1-52941-602-2
eBook ISBN 978-1-52941-603-9

10 9 8 7 6 5 4 3 2 1

Design by Tokiko Morishima
Cover and interior artwork by Romy Palstra

MIX
Paper from
responsible sources
FSC® C008047

Printed in China

the Joy of Baking

For my Dad

Contents

Introduction

I would never have believed that I would be worthy of writing a book, and yet here I am staring at a blank page, ready to embark on my own little magical writing journey. Despite a distinct sense of imposter syndrome, I am truly honoured to have been given the opportunity to share some of my experiences, the knowledge I have gained in the context of mental health and baking and, fundamentally, the joy to be obtained from throwing shapes in your kitchen.

I hope to take you on a mini journey of enlightenment; woven between these pages are messages of hope, strength and happiness. This isn't about producing perfect, patisserie-level bakes; it's about immersing yourself in the process, overcoming anxieties, nourishing yourself inside and out, and hopefully experiencing some incredible positive changes in your life as a result.

A Voyage to Baking Nirvana

Baking has become my comfort blanket. Since the age of 17, I have struggled to varying extents with diagnosed mental-health issues, but even before that, and for as long as I can remember, I have been anxious. I would cling to my mum's arm for dear life in unfamiliar environments; I was cautious and afraid. While I was relatively confident with people and in places I knew and trusted, I also lived in fear of letting anyone down, of doing the wrong thing and not being good enough. I was (and still am to a major extent) your typical people-pleaser and perfectionist; I crave love and external validation.

To this day, I am prone to chaotic behaviour; wild highs and lows. Despite being very in tune with my emotions, I haven't always been able to deal with them that well, and I guess the pressures of school, adolescence and navigating this scary world in my teens were the catalyst for my more serious mental-health problems. I struggled first with depression and subsequently an eating disorder. I remain a work in progress, I live with the issues and manage them to different degrees. I'm fortunate that I have an incredibly loving family; in particular my dear mum who has been my rock throughout, but it would be lying to say it has been plain sailing, or to pretend I am 'cured'.

Where does the baking come in? Well, early on, I became preoccupied with food; at first exercising huge control, quickly followed by periods of feeling extremely out of control. Nevertheless, I remained fixated on what I consumed. Initially I would try to prepare healthy meals and snacks – things that felt safe; knowing that the ingredients were nourishing made the process somewhat cathartic, and the outcome more acceptable to eat.

Sometime later, and following the death of my wonderful grandpa, I channelled this food obsession as well as grief over the loss of my hero into creating one of his greatest loves, good-quality bread. Progressively, my interest in baking and food evolved beyond things that were deemed 'healthy' to include those that were technical, varied and wholesome, as well as foods that I would otherwise have considered 'out of bounds' – wonderful crusty bread, rich cakes laced in frosting, sweet soft-baked cookies and puddings drowned in custard. As clichéd as it sounds, I started to heal a little bit with each and every bake.

'Even the Dreams You Haven't Dreamed Yet Can Come True

What started out as a distraction became a healthy obsession. I found myself in the kitchen almost every day exploring the world of baking. Moreover, I found it an incredibly calming pastime. It silenced the intrusive thoughts; occupied me in a way that felt creative and rewarding; it excited me, relaxed me and instilled some confidence; it gave me life, hope and pure joy.

Some 18 months after I had discovered the wonder of baking, I found myself in a tent in Berkshire being judged by baking royalty on *The Great British Bake Off*. While the experience was incredibly nerve-racking at times, I was, and still am, filled with nothing but gratitude for being able to share, through baked goods, my journey, my creativity and my desire to spread love and kindness always. My success on the show means very little; what I will forever be proud of was my ability to face doubt, anxiety and fear, confront my demons and share my passion with others.

Back to the Book...

I'm not a psychologist or an expert baker and this is not a self-help book. It isn't written backed by extensive studies and research – I happen to be extremely interested in science and have read a lot, but I'm a million miles from being able to advise professionally on matters, either from a mental-health perspective or a baking perspective. I simply love to learn and thus share what I have learned with others in the hope that it may empower them too. Among the following pages is a little wisdom, and a selection of my favourite bakes – hopefully a few that will catch your eye.

Let the kitchen become your playground, your safe space to explore the world as you did when you were a child – with exuberance, imagination and curiosity. I'm not saying that this book can provide the answers to everything that life throws at us, but I hope that it can give you a little courage to embrace the moment, linger in gratitude, acknowledge your greatness and, ultimately, live a more contented life.

Baking for Calm

Ask people why they bake and almost every response you get back is 'I find it calming' or 'I do it to relax, to switch off and unwind', and I'm in full agreement. The kitchen has become my safe space and baking is my therapy. Be it a form of mindfulness and meditation first thing in the morning; a stress reliever after a day at work or when everything feels too much; an outlet and a way of coping with my emotions; a pastime that is purely for me, or simply for comfort and nostalgia's sake – it's my medicine.

> *'Stop trying to calm the storm,*
> *calm yourself, the storm will pass'*
>
> Timber Hawkeye

While I find baking a very calming activity, that is not to say my kitchen is a place free from baking mishap or the occasional kitchen meltdown – far from it! Just because it's my passion and just because I went on a baking show does NOT mean I know what I'm doing all of the time. I mean, I do know some things, but I'm not awash with technical knowledge. I learned a lot on *Bake Off* and in the couple of years since, but I have never had formal training, it's just been me bumbling along in my (mum's) little kitchen. On this basis, things go wrong FREQUENTLY, and more frequently than you would imagine! For every Instagram-worthy shot, there are about ten prior attempts that have led me to that point, unless we are talking sourdough, in which case, make it a hundred prior attempts!

As every baker will know, sometimes things simply don't work and that's just baking. This might sound the exact opposite of calm, but with every mistake I make, I learn something new; failure really does teach us so much more than success. Professionals don't get it right every time either, it's part of the 'thrill'. Therefore an element of baking requires you to anticipate slip-ups, embrace errors and consider each catastrophe to be the best lesson. With this positive view, you can't lose the sense of calm, meditation, escapism, self-care and comfort that baking generates... even when the outcome resembles a dog's dinner.

This chapter will touch on the different ways I seek calm from my baking. Firstly, I explore baking as a form of mindfulness, meditation and a way of cultivating positive lifestyle habits. On mornings when I don't have to be up and out of the house early for work, I wake up, stumble downstairs to the kitchen, brew a strong coffee and, more often than not, set about baking something – it's almost instinctive, a brain-protective mechanism. It's the time of day when I am fully in the moment; I feel like I am getting a head-start on the rest of the world – a baking elf, whipping up some magic while everyone else is still asleep. I can immerse myself in the process of whatever I set about doing: it's meditative.

Next, I touch on the stress relief and escapism that come with launching yourself into a fountain of flour. I also refer to the role baking can play in managing emotions. After a particularly bad night's sleep or a stressful day of work, I am known for habitually gravitating towards the kitchen and baking something. Call it procrastibaking, stress baking or anxiety baking, baking instils an immediate sense of calm; not only that, it often helps me organize my thoughts better and even solve the initial problem or task at hand.

I then examine how baking can help us to slow down. As someone who lives life at 100 miles an hour, I find it very difficult to stop...OK baking isn't stopping entirely, but taking on a bake that doesn't require pace, stress or concentration can be incredibly soothing.

In part four of this chapter, I talk about baking as self-care; when I bake, I am prioritizing my mental wellbeing, I forgo people-pleasing and concentrate on myself. We spend so much of our lives trying to please others, be they friends, family, colleagues or social media, we may find that we seldom think about pleasing or prioritizing ourselves. Sometimes though, I can find myself with a real desire for some peace or a particular indulgence... and in these moments, it's no longer about anyone else, it's all about ME.

Finally in this chapter, I seek the comfort that baking can provide. Be it the smell of spices or vanilla, or the aroma of freshly baked bread – I find myself contented and calm as I'm reminded of happy times or salivating at the thought of whatever it is I have baked. We can also gain comfort from the process and the preparation of ingredients, followed by the ability to share an all-time favourite with family and friends.

So, before I waffle on too much, pop the kettle on, grab an oh-so-calming chamomile tea and take yourself on a little discovery of baking calm in the next few pages.

14

Baking for Mindfulness and Meditation

I'm not very good at switching off; my brain just doesn't stop chatting. Sometimes I ask my mum or friends what they are thinking, and they will reply, 'Nothing', which frankly baffles me – aren't you always thinking? Needless to say, mindfulness and meditation, they don't come naturally to me.

Of course, I think I must be broken, and an epic failure – I mean, I can't even manage to just BE; that's all meditation is, isn't it? Sit still, exist in the moment, breathe. On the subject of breathing, I've tried that before too – I went through a period when I had a lot going on, I was stressed, anxious and worried. I'd read that focusing on my breath could help, so I gave it a bash…I kid you not, I spent about three weeks thereafter feeling this strange sort of breathless that nearly had me in A&E because I was so convinced I was dying. I still sometimes experience this breathless sensation, the difference is that now I can pretty much be sure it's just that I have a lot on my plate and am not taking enough rest.

Something I have learned recently though is that, actually I CAN be mindful and meditate, I just don't do it like everyone else does; instead, I bake. Maybe it's not what the rulebook would say is meditation, but I know what works for me. And when you think about it, different people will take different medicine for the same condition, they will also have different doses and so, what it comes down to is finding your medicine, the right dose and making sure you take it as necessary.

For me, a bread bake is most calming: first, in preparing the dough, you have to concentrate on the ingredients and the steps, and then the kneading, either by hand or in a stand mixer, just watching and waiting as the dough transforms from sticky and seemingly unmanageable to so smooth and elastic that it rivals some of those incredible stress balls you can buy. Next there is the waiting while it proves, which allows you to go about your routine, come back, do some shaping – as intricate and creative as you like – add a filling and later a glaze, even some icing for extra sparkle, and before you know it your moment of Zen has produced something utterly spectacular.

This recipe assumes some level of bread-baking experience. However, with practice comes perfection and, quite honestly, anyone can do it. Initially, I hated the stickiness of kneading dough – the process felt ALL wrong. With time, plenty of failures and a little perseverance, I found my way. Online video tutorials can also help you visualize techniques for kneading, including the slap and fold method devised by legendary baker Richard Bertinet.

This might not be your version of meditation medicine but it really works for me…and even if it doesn't work as a form of meditation for you, these buns are blooming awesome so be sure to have a go – they won't disappoint.

Cinnamon Buns

Makes 12 buns

Hands on time: 30–40 minutes
+ 3–4 hours proving time
Cooking time: 20–23 minutes

INGREDIENTS

Dough

250ml (8fl oz) whole milk
45g (1¾oz) runny honey
25g (1oz) extra virgin
olive oil
500g (1lb) strong white
bread flour,
plus extra for dusting
2 teaspoons ground
cardamom
2 teaspoons ground
cinnamon
7g (¼oz) sachet of fast-
action dried yeast
10g (½oz) fine sea salt
1 large egg, lightly beaten
35g (1¼oz) softened
unsalted butter, cubed

Filling

120g (3¾oz) unsalted
butter
120g (3¾oz) soft light
brown sugar
1 tablespoon ground
cinnamon

Glaze

25g (1oz) caster sugar
25g (1oz) water
Pinch of ground cinnamon
¼ teaspoon vanilla extract

Cream Cheese Frosting
(optional)

30g (1¼oz) softened
unsalted butter
35g (1¼oz) cream cheese
60g (2½oz) icing sugar,
sifted
Grated zest of ½ lemon

METHOD

In a jug or bowl gently heat the milk in the microwave for 20–30 seconds or until lukewarm, then add the honey and olive oil to the milk, stir and set aside.

Add the flour, ground cardamom and ground cinnamon to a large bowl and gently mix. Next add the yeast to one side of the bowl and the salt to the opposite side (see Recipe tips, page 21), followed by the egg, cubed butter and finally the milk mixture. Combine the ingredients using a spoon or your hands until it forms a cohesive dough.

Once fully combined, transfer to the work surface and knead for 10–12 minutes or until the dough is elastic and smooth – if you find the dough sticking, rub a little olive oil on your hands or onto the work surface.

Alternatively, use a stand mixer and mix the dough on a medium speed for around 10 minutes – this is my preferred method for this dough.

Transfer to a lightly oiled bowl, cover with clingfilm and leave in a warm environment for 2–3 hours or until doubled in size. An airing cupboard can be useful if your house is particularly cool in the winter months.

Prepare the filling. Beat the butter, sugar and cinnamon together for 2–3 minutes until light and fluffy.

Once the dough has doubled in size, punch the air out of it, before turning out onto a very lightly floured work surface. Using a rolling pin, roll the dough out to a rectangle approximately 40 × 50cm (16 × 20in), with the longest edge towards you.

Use a palette knife to spread the butter and sugar combo over the dough, taking it right to the edges. Tightly roll up the dough from one of the longest edges until you have a long cylindrical shape. Trim the untidy edges (these needn't go to waste, you can still bake them off on a separate tray) before dividing into 12 equal chunks – I use a measuring tape because 1. I can't judge by eye and 2. I'm a stickler for precision!

Transfer the 12 rolls spiral side up onto a 23 × 30cm (9 × 12in) baking tin (or approximate equivalent) lined with greaseproof paper. Cover loosely with clingfilm and leave to rise in the same warm environment for a further 1 hour or until approximately doubled in size.

Preheat the oven to 200°C (180°C fan/400°F/Gas Mark 6).

Next, prepare the glaze. Combine the sugar, water, cinnamon and vanilla in a small saucepan and place over a medium heat until the sugar has dissolved, then set aside.

Prepare the frosting if you are using it. Combine the butter, cream cheese and icing sugar in a bowl. Beat with a hand-held electric whisk to form a smooth mixture – don't

20

Recipe tips

- Salt can retard the activity of yeast so aim to keep the two on separate sides of the bowl in the initial mixing process.

- When kneading, use the window pane test to measure the gluten development in the dough – pinch a small lump of dough, stretch out all four corners and check for a smooth, translucent window. This means the dough is ready to rise.

- If you have a stand mixer, it can be helpful in the initial stages of bread baking, simply to understand how the dough feels and the changes that occur as a result of gluten formation (i.e. kneading).

overbeat. Add the lemon zest before briefly beating one final time. Cover with clingfilm until ready to use.

Once the buns have risen, remove the clingfilm, and place in the preheated oven for 20–23 minutes. They should be golden brown when baked.

Remove from the oven, lightly brush with the glaze and transfer to a cooling rack. If you are using the frosting, spread or pipe a small amount on top of the buns once they are fully cooled. Enjoy.

Baking for Stress Relief

Rather embarrassingly, I am pretty prone to tantrums; there are times when I just can't seem to cope with how I feel. It's like there is all this energy in my head, it isn't happy and it doesn't know how to respond…so I take it out on things (including humans) that are in my firing line. Yup, people, WATCH OUT – I've Frisbeed cookies at my best friend, mashed lemon mousse into my mum's hair, peeled the sticky letters off our expensive piano (admittedly, this was when I was about seven and having to endure piano lessons, which I hated) but you get the gist: I can be a bit of a storm in a teacup.

When I took to bread baking…it proved (excuse the pun) to be a mini miracle in helping me handle my emotions. Granted, the effects were sometimes temporary, but I could really punch the life out of a piece of dough. It wasn't remotely destructive and it allowed me to release some of my energy and, if I managed to sustain enough patience and concentration to carry me through the next few phases, it resulted in a pretty pleasing outcome.

However, there are several risks when it comes to baking while you're in an almighty funk and experience tells me it's not worth dabbling with jeopardy when you're already somewhat volatile. First off, avoid precision baking: when you've managed to convince yourself in no uncertain terms that you can't possibly finish that assignment for work or that your beautifully structured day has been unceremoniously obliterated, the likelihood of your head managing to stand up to precise measurements and intricate detail is slim...so just don't go there. Second, I find that when I'm baking in this state, it's as much about the process as it is the outcome; the physical outlet of pummelling a lump of dough is the therapy, the rewarding outcome is the extra sprinkles. A lengthy, less labour-intensive process just doesn't seem to hit the spot and, worse still, can leave you feeling even more drained and frustrated, so, again, leave that for another day.

I find everything about bread pleasing and, in terms of being able to fulfil multiple requirements, this flatbread is a winner. It's versatile, pretty forgiving and the end result is enough to make you feel like you've created something worthy of a Michelin star.

Three-way Flat Breads

**Makes 4 pizzas,
10–12 pittas,
10–12 flatbreads**

Hands on time: 30 minutes
+ 2–3 hours proving time
Cooking time: pizzas 20 minutes,
pittas 15 minutes,
flatbreads 45 minutes

INGREDIENTS

Dough

500g (1lb) white bread
flour, plus
extra for dusting
10g (½oz) caster sugar
7g (¼ oz) sachet of fast-
action dried yeast
1 teaspoon fine sea salt
300ml (½ pint) tepid water
20ml (1fl oz) extra virgin
olive oil
Semolina, for dusting
(optional)

Tomato Sauce

400g (13oz) can of plum
tomatoes (San Marzano
are the best)
1 tablespoon olive oil
½ teaspoon dried oregano
Small bunch of basil

Toppings

140g (5oz) mozzarella
20g (¾oz) Parmesan
Handful of basil leaves, plus
extra for garnishing

METHOD

Combine the flour and sugar in a large bowl. Add the yeast to one side of the bowl and the salt to the opposite side (see Recipe tips, page 21).

Mix the water and olive oil in a jug, then add to the flour mixture and combine to form a dough. Tip onto the work surface and knead for 8–10 minutes until smooth and elastic. (If you find the dough sticking, rub a little olive oil on your hands or onto the work surface.) Transfer to a lightly oiled bowl, cover with clingfilm or a clean tea towel, and leave to prove in a warm environment for 1–2 hours or until doubled in size (see Recipe tips, page 27).

Once risen, tip onto a very lightly floured surface.

TO MAKE PIZZAS

Punch the air out of the dough, and divide into 4. If you're keen to be precise, weigh the full quantity of dough and divide by 4 – it should be approximately 200g (7oz) per portion of dough.

Take 1 portion of dough and form into a tight ball as follows: using both hands, which remain in contact with the work surface, cup the side of the dough farthest from you and gently drag the dough down towards your body, creating tension on the outside of the dough. Rotate the dough using both hands and perform another gentle drag towards your body. Continue rotating and dragging in this way until the dough is sufficiently taut and uniformly round.

Repeat for the remaining 3 portions of dough. Rest covered with a clean, damp tea towel for another 1 hour.

Meanwhile prepare the sauce. Drain the tomatoes of their juices and combine in a bowl with the olive oil and oregano. Blitz together using a stick blender or, for a chunkier sauce, scrunch with your fingers or a fork. Briefly bash the basil leaves with the back of a knife or pestle before placing in the sauce to infuse. Set aside at room temperature.

Once rested, transfer the first ball of dough to a floured rimless baking sheet or a chopping board liberally dusted with flour or semolina (see Recipe tips, page 27).

Shape the dough: using both hands press down and gently stretch the dough in a uniform fashion into a pizza approximately 25cm (10in) in size. Start at the side of the dough farthest from you and work towards your body. You want to keep your hands flat with the dough. Try not to press out any air at the rim of the dough where the edge will form – you want this to rise up as high as possible.

Top the pizza with a scant smear of the tomato sauce (be careful not to add too much or you will end up with a soggy pizza), followed by a quarter of the mozzarella, a quarter of the Parmesan and a few basil leaves.

Recipe tips

- If you can get hold of it, use 00 flour (a wheat flour typically milled in Italy) for your pizza dough to create a more authentically Italian pizza.

- Sprinkling semolina on your chopping board helps the dough to slide off and into the frying pan easily.

- For a pizza with even more flavour, transfer the dough to the fridge for the initial prove, leaving for at least 8 hours and up to 24 hours.

- Use a firm mozzarella or even the grated stuff – the superior 'buffalo' varieties are often creamier and contain more water that can lead to a soggy dough.

Heat a heavy-based frying pan with an ovenproof handle on high until it's smoking hot. And preheat the grill on high.

Carefully slide the pizza off the baking sheet or board into the pan. Cook for around 3 minutes – or until lightly charred when you peek underneath – before popping under the grill for another 2 minutes – keep an eye on it. The edges will puff up and char slightly and the cheese will be melted and bubbly. Remove the pan from the grill and carefully slide the pizza out onto a chopping board.

Rest for about 5 minutes (if you can) before tucking in. Safety warning…melted cheese is bound to burn the roof of your mouth but is SO worth it.

Repeat to make the remaining pizzas.

TO MAKE PITTAS

After the initial prove, place a pizza stone or baking tray in the oven and preheat to 250°C (230°C fan/500°F/Gas Mark 9).

Punch the air out of the dough and divide into 10–12 balls, each weighing around 70g (3oz). Cover with a clean tea towel for around 20 minutes.

Dust your work surface with flour and, using a rolling pin, gently roll each ball into an oval or slipper shape about 1cm (½ in) thick. Rest for another 5 minutes.

If using a pizza stone, carefully transfer each portion of dough onto the stone. I can usually get about 3–4 on at once. Alternatively, remove the baking tray from the oven, transfer 3–4 pittas onto the tray and immediately put it back into the oven. Cook for 4–5 minutes or until puffed up and very lightly golden on top.

Remove from the oven and transfer to a cooling rack, covering with a clean, dry tea towel to keep them soft. Repeat the process until all of the dough is used up.

TO MAKE FLATBREADS

After the initial prove, punch the air out of the dough,
and divide into 10–12 balls, each weighing around
70g (3oz). Cover with a clean tea towel and rest for
20 minutes.

Preheat a heavy-based frying pan on a high heat.

Dust your work surface with flour and, using a rolling
pin, roll the dough balls into rough circles, about 5mm
(¼in) thick. Rest for another couple of minutes before
placing one flatbread in the smoking hot pan. Cook for
90 seconds–2 minutes on one side. Check for a few
charred spots appearing on the underside, then carefully
flip and cook for another couple of minutes. Once cooked,
transfer to a cooling rack and cover with a clean, dry tea
towel. Repeat for the remaining dough portions.

The Art of
Slowing
Down

I distinctly remember a conversation with my grandma, at the tender age of ten, when she asked me what I wanted to be when I grew up. My reply was, 'I just want to drink tea and eat scones.' I clearly had great aspirations and I'm quite sure she put her head in her hands in despair following our discussion! Despite being too young to really acknowledge the significance of this statement, I now think I had a very good point, and I still (somewhat) stand by what I said. I just wish for a simple life, one that feels cosy, safe and content and involves friends, family and special moments. I guess a scone, clotted cream, jam and a cup of tea epitomize this for me.

Scones have also been pretty significant during my mental-health journey. I can remember very specific circumstances that followed a similar pattern: I'd either be feeling really low, or stressed, or it was cold and miserable, occasionally I'd have had a medical appointment and, for whatever reason, lunch hadn't happened. I'd end up in a café – more often than not with Mum. I'd sit there needing something else to concentrate on, something that wasn't the uncomfortable emotions or physical feelings. I'd opt for a scone; sometimes with fruit, sometimes plain, ALWAYS with clotted cream and strawberry jam and, for that sweet moment, I was taken off to a place of calm, contentment and peace.

So, you get it, scones are a good thing in my book, yet I came out of the *Bake Off* tent having never made one! Simple, I thought. Well yes... unless you are a perfectionist like me. I have now sampled more scones than I care to remember. Don't worry, I haven't lost my love for them. My issue was that each time I followed a recipe it didn't quite match those that I remembered from my past. However, after much trial and error, some science and geekery, I believe I have come up with something really quite special. It's rich and buttery, fluffy and moist and just crying out for some wicked clotted cream and jam.

Besides the very pleasing outcome, there is also something incredibly therapeutic about the process of baking a batch of scones. It's the perfect combination: a slow, calming and mindful process that yields a relatively quick outcome – perfect if, like me, you get bored easily.

You don't need to think too hard, just follow the recipe and let your mind wander… it takes time to rub the butter into the flour, you have to focus a bit but not too much. Worries seem to temporarily evaporate, and I find that my creativity and imagination are enlivened.

Then it gets a bit messy; sometimes at this stage you might think it's gone wrong but don't worry, remain calm and persevere, and now it's a short waiting game interspersed with stamping out little rounds of dough and remembering to pop the oven on before lobbing them in and, yes, watching them as they rise. Staring at my oven door has become a regular pastime, it's science right before my eyes and as the bake does (or doesn't do) what it's supposed to do, I stare in wonder and often disbelief.

This all sounds quite profound. It really isn't, and in fact, before writing this book, I don't think I've ever really acknowledged my emotions and feelings while I bake… I just know it feels good, the brain chatter switches from destructive to productive, I have a purpose, and, before long, I can appreciate and share my efforts. Put simply, it makes me happy.

Scones

....

Makes 8–10 scones   **Hands-on time:** 15 minutes +
                           1 hour 20 minutes resting time
                           Cooking time: 12–15 minutes

....

INGREDIENTS

80g (3oz) thick double cream
120g (3¾oz) buttermilk
2 teaspoons fresh lemon
  juice
300g (10oz) plain flour, plus
  extra for dusting and
  dredging
55g (2oz) caster sugar
10g (½oz) baking powder
Pinch of salt
55g (2oz) unsalted butter,
  cubed (cold but pliable)
1 egg yolk, beaten

To Serve
Strawberry jam
Clotted cream

METHOD

Combine the cream, buttermilk and lemon juice in a
jug and leave for approximately 20 minutes – the mixture
may curdle slightly, this is fine.

Place the flour, sugar, baking powder and salt in a
large bowl. Add the cubed butter and use your fingertips
to rub it into the flour mixture until it resembles breadcrumbs.

33

Add the buttermilk mixture to the dry ingredients and combine using a wooden spoon until it comes together to form a rough dough. Don't worry if the mixture seems quite dry, just gently bring it together as best you can. Tip onto a lightly floured work surface and lightly knead for around 30 seconds to form a cohesive dough. Cover with clingfilm and rest for around 30 minutes.

Once the dough is rested, remove from the clingfilm, pop onto a lightly floured work surface and, using your hands, flatten to form a disc around 2cm (¾in) thick. Coat a 6cm (2½in) round cutter with flour and stamp out rounds. Pop on a baking tray lined with baking parchment. Gently remould any remaining dough and keep stamping out rounds until it's all used up. Cover the scones with clingfilm and rest for a further 30 minutes.

Preheat the oven to 200°C (180°C fan/400°F/Gas Mark 6) and pop a second large baking tray in the oven to preheat.

Variations
Add 85g (3¼oz) dried fruit – sultanas or dried sour cherries are my preference – or 120g (3¾oz) fresh blueberries and the zest of 1 lemon to the dry ingredients and mix through before adding the wet ingredients. The dough can be a bit trickier to handle but don't panic, it will come together and taste great.

Once rested, remove the clingfilm from the scones and brush the tops with the beaten egg yolk. Remove the preheated baking tray from the oven and carefully transfer the baking parchment and scones onto the preheated tray. Bake for 12–15 minutes or until lightly golden on top.

Remove from the oven, transfer to a cooling rack and allow to cool before adding a dollop of clotted cream and jam...in whichever order you prefer!

Recipe tips

- To make your own buttermilk, add 10ml (1 dessertspoon) lemon juice to 120ml (4fl oz) whole milk and set aside for around 20 minutes; it should thicken a bit, and that's it – it's then ready to use.

- Preheating your baking tray as directed is not essential but it can help boost the rise of the scones.

Baking for
Self-Care

I worry a lot, and people who know me well would say that's an understatement. It's often one simple thought that spreads like wildfire and suddenly becomes an almighty mountain of a problem.

For this reason, I spend a lot of time trying to make sure I do things for other people: presents, bakes, posts on social media, replying personally to direct messages, emails. Some of this is an avoidance tactic – I distract my mind from the worry by focusing on other people; at other times it's because I want to make people happy, which can help me feel happy, and sometimes it's all about external validation and seeking approval – if someone else says I've done good, I can be a little more satisfied that I might actually have done OK.

What all this comes down to is learning to love, respect and appreciate myself without the need for approval from others. You've probably heard this before and are thinking 'Go on then, how have you done it?' Well I'm not sure I have – certainly not consistently; but I guess acknowledging this is part of the battle. More recently,

I have learned to accept that fragile mental health is part of my make-up. Like any chronic condition, I have to learn to live with it and not expect that it will necessarily ever be 'fixed'.

When I was younger, I held the somewhat unrealistic perception that therapy was about overcoming a problem, becoming a normal person and living happily ever after. Call me a cynic, but I'm just not sure this is realistic. However, what I have learned is how to better manage my mental health through simple self-care. A series of seemingly inconsequential habits – some of which I would never have acknowledged as being valuable at the time – have led me to where I am today: more stable, self-aware, insightful and informed.

I never set about baking because I thought it was going to make me feel better mentally, but what I now realize is that it forces me to engage in positive practices. It's my version of self-care. I forgo the face masks, pedicures and

spa days, sport a fetching monobrow 90 per cent of the time, as well as a smear of eyeliner across my cheek and, as a result of my baking exploits, quite often look like I've been rolling around in food products for most of the day, but when I set about baking, I immediately feel calmer and a little happier. It's not about pleasing others, just me and my needs.

In this instance, a perfect bake is one that is fairly simple, maybe with a few little achievable steps involved, one that provides comfort at the end of it and that isn't about aesthetics or feeding a family of eight. My great-grandma apparently used to cook and bake, like many women of her generation, and it strikes me she was pretty blooming good at it. Sadly, I never got to enjoy her bakes, but her recipes remain in my mum's tatty little recipe book and so the legend lives on! This bread and butter pudding recipe is a take on hers: SO simple in flavour, an excellent use of stale bread and a purely comforting pud. My version is a single serve, the ultimate manifestation of a self-care bake encouraging you to indulge in creating something delicious for just yourself to enjoy. You can be really engaged in the process while making it, be as precise or slapdash as you wish, and the only person who can moan is you.

The recipe is for two mini single-serve puddings; I make one and freeze the other for when I need an immediate B&B hit.

Single-serve Bread and Butter Pud

Makes 2 puddings   **Hands on time:** 15 minutes +
                              20–30 minutes soaking time
                              Cooking time: 25 minutes

INGREDIENTS

100g (3½oz) white bread, cut about 1cm (½in) thick
30g (1¼oz) unsalted softened butter, plus extra
   for greasing
15g (½oz) golden caster sugar
15g (½oz) demerara sugar
1 teaspoon mixed spice
40g (1½oz) sultanas
Grated zest of 1 small lemon
200ml (7fl oz) whole milk
1 egg, lightly whisked

METHOD

Grease 2 small dishes – round or square, around 9cm
(3½in) in diameter/width. Preheat the oven to 170°C
(150°C fan/350°F/Gas Mark 4).

Remove any thick crusts from the bread – you should
have around 80g (3oz) remaining. Spread both sides of the
bread with the butter and slice into 'soldiers'.

**Tightly arrange a layer of the bread neatly over the
base of each dish** – you may need to trim a few bits to
ensure there aren't any gaps. If your dish is round, just

curve the bread to fit snugly
in the dish.

Combine the two sugars.
For each dish: sprinkle
a quarter of the sugar
mixture over the bread
layer, followed by
¼ teaspoon of the mixed
spice, half the sultanas and
a quarter of the lemon zest.

Next place another layer of bread into the dishes.
Distribute the remaining mixed spice, sugar mixture and
lemon zest evenly over the top of each dish.

Whisk the milk and lightly whisked egg in a large jug
so that the two are well combined. Pour the liquid mixture
evenly over the layered bread in each dish until it just
submerges the bread. You are likely to have a little too
much liquid. I find that once it has soaked in a bit, you can
add a little more. Approximately 90–100ml (3¼–3 ½fl oz)
of the liquid per dish seems to work for me – this will vary
a bit depending on the size of your dish.

Leave to soak for 20–30 minutes before placing in the
oven for approximately 25 minutes. The pudding is ready
when it is golden brown on top and the milk and egg
mixture has puffed up a bit.

Baking for Comfort

I believe baking, and actually, food in general, can be incredibly calming when there is real meaning attached to it. A bake or the act of baking, a flavour, smell, texture that takes you back to a time when you were particularly happy can induce the same degree of relaxation and calm in the present time.

If you have picked up this book, I'm guessing you have, at some point in your life, been affected by mental health, or maybe you just want to recapture the joy in baking that has been dimmed by rush, stress and busyness. In either case, there may well be a time in the past that you can think back to when your brain seemed to function more optimally than it does now.

When I look back on my youth, prior to suffering acutely with depression and an eating disorder, I recall being a pretty anxious kid; I worried about trivia, hated change and lacked confidence. I vividly remember running upstairs each morning before school and hiding under my bed with my fingers in my ears while Mum started the car – we had a temperamental Peugeot 205 that tended to not start and for some reason this worried me a LOT. Therefore, to a certain extent, I sense that my mental health has always been precarious; it's part of my genetic make-up and it simply took the flick of a switch around the age of 16 to catapult me from functioning pretty well, to very much not coping and needing some help.

The fundamental difference was that at this time I lost the ability to have fun, laugh a proper belly laugh, be excited about things or daydream amazing possibilities and scenarios. This numb sensation will be familiar to anyone who has suffered with depression or anxiety. I began to approach things with fear, anticipate the worst, think up every eventuality possible of things that could go wrong and, in all honestly, I still don't think I have regained a complete level of life fulfilment.

It seems, however, that reminiscing about times of old can be a wonderful tool for calming my mind, even making me smile that little 'OMG I remember that' smile. I'm talking about the good old moments: giggling myself silly with my friends in Art when we taped masking-tape boobs onto our teacher's apron; sitting in Cuba on a sunbed perched in the sea, watching the sunset and sipping on Mum's piña colada; dressing up for the school disco in my pink octopus pants (tell me you remember these?), sparkly top and even some EYELINER – such a grown-up; having friends over and making a den; eating Skittles with Dad at the orange swings (named because they were orange… and the 'other' swings presumably weren't orange).

It turns out reminiscence therapy is an actual thing, the aim of which is to find meaning in memories. It is a common therapy for those suffering from dementia and can be used to improve self-esteem. Reminiscence therapy is broadly defined as a treatment that uses all of the senses, and I can relate to this. While it's great recalling nice memories, the comfort often fades quite quickly. However, I find baking – with its evocation of all the senses – really maximizes the reward.

Generally baking that engages this mindset is centred around the bake itself: it should be relevant to you and your life, something that sparks happy memories. Similarly, though, just the activity – for example, weighing out ingredients or kneading dough – can take you back to a time in your past when you engaged in the same activity with particular joy; like that one time when I whipped cream to pipe onto a pavlova and somehow managed to end up with cream on the ceiling, myself and the walls…I have photo evidence if you are interested and, yes, there was plenty of laughter involved too! Even creating something purely because the smell is reminiscent of a wonderful time; THAT coffee cake that grandma use to make which perfumed the house for HOURS afterwards. Whatever you can remember making you happy, go make it!

Alternatively, you can make my version of a nostalgic bake – school cherry crumble. I've brought it into the 21st century with desiccated coconut and a touch of lemon zest, it really is a game-changer!

Cherry and Coconut Crumble

Serves 4–6

Hands on time: 15 minutes +
10–15 minutes chilling time
Cooking time: 30–35 minutes

INGREDIENTS

Cherry Filling
1 × 400g (13oz) bag of dark
  frozen cherries
20g (¾oz) golden caster
  sugar
Squeeze of fresh lemon
  juice and zest of ½ lemon

Crumble
80g (3oz) spelt wheat flour
50g (2oz) coconut oil
¼ teaspoon salt
40g (1½oz) soft light
  brown sugar
50g (2oz) rolled oats
20g (¾oz) desiccated
  coconut
½ tablespoon ice-cold
  water

Quick Vanilla Custard
600ml (1 pint) whole milk
1 teaspoon vanilla bean
  paste
4 egg yolks
30g (1¼oz) caster sugar
1 tablespoon cornflour

METHOD

Approximately 1 hour prior to baking, transfer the cherries to a bowl and allow to defrost. Preheat the oven to 200°C (180°C fan/400°F/Gas Mark 6).

Next, prepare the crumble. Rub the flour and coconut oil together with your fingertips to create a fine breadcrumb-like mixture. Stir through the salt, brown sugar, oats and desiccated coconut. Finally, drizzle over the ice-cold water and use a knife to cut through the mixture; it should form a few little nuggets – you can use your hands to squeeze the mixture together a little more if you like your crumble nicely clustered. Transfer to the fridge for 10–15 minutes to firm up a little.

Drain the liquid off the defrosted cherries and transfer to an ovenproof dish approximately 20 x 14cm (8 x 6in). Add the sugar, lemon juice and zest and stir to combine.

Top the fruit with the crumble and pop in the preheated oven for around 30–35 minutes or until bubbling and golden brown on top.

While the crumble is cooking, prepare the custard. Add the milk and vanilla to a saucepan, place over a medium heat and slowly bring to the boil, stirring periodically. Meanwhile, pop the egg yolks, caster sugar and cornflour in large bowl and whisk together to form a thin paste.

When the vanilla milk has just come to the boil, add a third to the egg mixture, whisking continuously. Tip this mixture back into the pan of remaining vanilla milk and, over a low heat, whisk until the mixture thickens slightly. Pour into a jug and serve at once with the steaming cherry crumble!

Variations

For an alternative fruit dessert, simply bake your favourite fruit in the oven at around 190°C (170°C fan/375°F/Gas Mark 5) for 25–30 minutes or until the fruit begins to soften a little. My favourites are:

- Stone and halve 400g (13oz) of plums and arrange skin side down in an ovenproof dish. Add 70ml (2½fl oz) orange juice, zest of ½ orange, 1 cinnamon stick, 2 star anise, 1–2 cubes of chopped crystallized ginger, ½ teaspoon of vanilla extract and a teaspoon or two of sugar, to taste.

- Stone and halve 400g (13oz) of fresh apricots or peaches, arrange skin side down in an ovenproof dish. Add 50ml (2fl oz) orange juice, 1 tablespoon amaretto, zest of ½ orange, ½ teaspoon of vanilla extract and a sprinkle of sugar.

Meanwhile, prepare the crumble topping as described in the main recipe. Spread over a large baking tray and bake in the oven for 10–15 minutes at 200°C (180°C fan/400°F/Gas Mark 6) or until golden brown. Top the baked fruit with a layer of the crunchy crumble. (Freeze any leftovers and use as a topping for future baked fruit, porridge or yogurt.)

- Swap the desiccated coconut with finely chopped hazelnuts or almonds and replace the coconut oil with unsalted butter for a different flavour crumble.

Baking for Focus

I believe that baking has benefits which can suit any situation – big or small. Sometimes, it's as simple as needing to switch off from a moment of feeling overwhelmed by the jumble of life. In other instances the negative emotions can be deeper rooted, requiring a vast shift of focus. Baking has the power to deal with all of this; it can switch one's attention, provide an outlet for creativity and it can reward, motivate and inspire.

> *'Yesterday is history, tomorrow is*
> *a mystery, today's a gift, that's why*
> *it's called the present'*

I turned to baking with real enthusiasm during a period of quite bad depression. It became a source of stress relief, focus and satisfaction. The process was organic, stemming largely from a preoccupation with food, control and a need to feel fulfilled. Contrary to what fairy tales make us believe, there wasn't an overnight epiphany, and I wouldn't say I lived happily ever after. No, as with everything I do, it was all pretty understated.

I was in a relatively dark place. That place exactly? Imagine the heaviest, greyest of days, you don't have a job that fulfils you, you're making no effort to feel good about yourself, you're engaging in negative behaviours; no, not sex, drugs and rock and roll, but too much caffeine, Diet Coke, late-night social media scrolling, lack of sleep and chronic self-comparison. To put it plainly, I was so sad it hurt. I cried helplessly and frequently, and I had no energy to do anything, let alone be 'happy'.

In the eye of this storm though, I found interest in watching people create nice food. I had followed food programmes for years; I grew up with *Ready Steady Cook*, and had since turned to *Bake Off* and *MasterChef* with greater interest, but I had never thought to try making food myself. Bread was my impetus to have a go, but my first flings with baking were somewhat fleeting and not always positively motivated – concocting 'healthy' bakes was a response to my eating disorder, controlled, calculated and obsessive. Then, gradually over this bleak period of a few months, I started to throw myself into proper buttery, sugary, glutenous baking, with increased interest and ultimately huge contentment.

I had always struggled to control the onslaught of chaotic emotions in my brain, yet, where baking was involved, I could utilize my brain energy more effectively. Instead of calculating calories, I could calculate percentages of ingredients; instead of obsessing over my own health and the science of my brain and body, I would spend time reading about the science of baking.

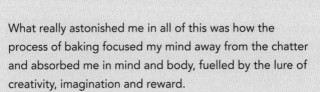

What really astonished me in all of this was how the process of baking focused my mind away from the chatter and absorbed me in mind and body, fuelled by the lure of creativity, imagination and reward.

The more people I meet in the culinary world, the more I realize I'm not alone in my relationship with baking. Multiple contestants from *Bake Off* alone have reported the benefits of baking for mental health, and author Marian Keyes documented her battle with depression and the power of baking in helping to lift her mood in her book *Saved by Cake*. While scientific studies into the benefits of baking are currently lacking, increasingly this is emerging as a new area of focus for psychologists and researchers of positive psychology who see the rich potential of baking as a focused activity that promotes creativity and self-expression as well as connection with others through sharing the food we make.[1]

This chapter explores the ways in which the focus involved in baking can help to divert the mind, allowing you to switch off from the hustle and bustle of life. Baking offers an opportunity to gain perspective and clarity but it's a careful balance between engaging in something focused enough to distract your mind, but not something too complex that it's destined for failure. Indeed, the importance of striking this balance is backed up by science. Positive psychologist Mihaly Csikszentmihalyi first coined the term 'flow' to describe a challenging but achievable task that requires complete concentration. Numerous studies have confirmed the importance of experiencing this kind of focused creative activity in our day-to-day lives for greater contentment and wellbeing.

A key element of flow is concentration, and baking also helps to concentrate the mind; an appreciation of the science behind baking encourages patience and an acceptance that, often, the best results come down to nature, nurture and science working their magic in unison. Sometimes, baking is about letting things develop at their own pace and all you can do is observe.

With my growing interest in baking, I have found myself gravitating towards the kitchen during moments of anxiety. Nowadays, I see this as a form of therapy – it shifts my focus and breaks the vicious cycle. Because of the spontaneous nature of these bakes, they are generally 'foraged' from things I have lurking in the kitchen. This also presents an opportunity to consider the environment and minimizing food waste. For me, this provides even more motivation to produce something epic, as well as allowing my baking to become a creative outlet. Playing with flavour combinations and textures, along with the aesthetic of a bake – there really are no limits: bread scoring, cake decorating, icing biscuits or assembling refined and stunning French pastries – you can go wild. The whole process is expressive, yet focused and ultimately extremely meditative.

Now if you're anything like me, I'm pretty sure you won't have focused long enough to read through all that waffle, so just go and delve into the next few pages – at the very least, there are some yummy bakes to try.

Switching Off from the Hustle and Bustle

Do you ever feel overwhelmed by life? The news, responsibilities, work…even family and friends can become demanding. I often find myself so deafened by the noise that I end up hiding from everything. Instead of approaching things rationally and piecemeal, I simply try to avoid it all (incidentally, this isn't a tactic I would advocate – it turns out that burying your head doesn't get you very far!).

I frequently find myself with countless unread WhatsApp messages, an inbox full of 'important' emails that haven't been actioned, Instagram messages that (embarrassingly) date back to about two years ago, and then of course, missed calls from friends and family. The irony of situations like these is that all this overwhelm comes with huge associated guilt, only perpetuated by continued avoidance of the issues at hand.

While there is always a logical way to approach circumstances like these, I find that when I feel frazzled I don't possess a particularly rational mindset. Thus, my approach is to just walk away from the world and re-emerge when I'm ready.

As you are probably beginning to gather, baking is an immediate source of respite for me. However, when I feel consumed with anxiety, I tend to bake a bit haphazardly. I will merrily start on something without much prior planning – which obviously carries some risk…the biggest being one almighty baking catastrophe. With that in mind, I have learnt to opt for things that are relatively robust to mishaps. On the flipside, I like to immerse myself in something that involves some degree of focus; properly engaging my brain and distracting it from the hustle and bustle.

A recipe that includes multiple ingredients and a number of achievable stages is perfect: something that requires sufficient mental capacity to distract me from reality but not so much that I'm open to risk. I also like a bake that can easily be modified. Then I can inject some creativity, be a little imaginative and even produce something novel and quite brilliant. This recipe is just that; the ingredients themselves can be interchanged with similar alternatives: hazelnuts, cashews or peanuts instead of pecans; try sultanas, dried cherries, mixed peel; switch orange zest for lemon, or go for ginger instead of cinnamon – you're the boss. Each element also takes a little preparation – roasting the nuts, chopping the dried fruit, zesting the orange, then combining them all methodically before rolling, cutting and baking. Yet you can't go far wrong with this one and, when you do, the result isn't disastrous.

Then the really mindful bit: prior to *Bake Off* I had never used a piping bag and nozzle. I'd watched others do it on YouTube and, because of their proficiency, was confident I'd be up to it. Obviously, I had to quickly acquaint myself with the process once things progressed with my application for the show and I immediately realized that it wasn't remotely as easy as it appeared. However, after some initial frustration, I fell in love with it. I spent one entire afternoon – well into the evening – icing biscuits. I must have been stood in my kitchen for about five hours amid a morass of piping bags containing icing of various colours and small piles of iced gingerbread biscuits gradually improving in quality with each attempt. The focus was huge but not demanding, just pure Zen.

Now, there is a drawback in the fact that I'm not a massive fan of the flavour or texture of icing in this form. It has its place in baking, which is purely decorative in my opinion. So, for this recipe I have found a biscuit that is far superior paired with chocolate and you can experience the same, if not greater, reward with the process of smoothing silky white chocolate over the base of each biscuit, piping

contrasting dark chocolate on top and then fashioning an impressive feathered effect.

After a suitable length of time distracted from reality, you can sit down, with a cup of tea and a biscuit, feeling a touch less overwhelmed and maybe even ready to try 'adulting' once more. If not, you've made a cracking biscuit and can be very proud of your efforts – it's a win-win.

Double Chocolate Feathered Spiced Biscuits

Makes 15–18 biscuits   **Hands on time: 20–30 minutes**

Cooking time: 25 minutes

INGREDIENTS

50g (2oz) pecans

75g (3oz) softened unsalted butter

30g (1¼oz) caster sugar

½ teaspoon vanilla extract

Zest of 1 large clementine or ½ an orange

40g (1½oz) dried cranberries

45g (1¾oz) plain flour, plus extra for dusting

30g (1¼oz) wholemeal flour

50g (2oz) oats

¼ teaspoon ground cinnamon

Pinch of salt

To Decorate

100g (3½oz) white chocolate

50g (2oz) dark chocolate

METHOD

Preheat the oven to 200°C (180°C fan/400°F/Gas Mark 6). Place the pecans on a small baking tray and roast for 8 minutes – keep an eye on them, don't let them burn. Once toasted and golden, remove from the oven, chop finely and set aside to cool. Lower the oven temperature to 190°C (170°C fan/375°F/Gas Mark 5).

Beat together the butter, sugar, vanilla and clementine or orange zest until light and fluffy – this will take around 2–3 minutes. Then finely chop the cranberries into small pieces.

In a separate bowl, mix together the flours, oats, cinnamon and salt until well combined. Once the pecans have cooled, add to the dry ingredients, followed by the cranberries and stir through to evenly distribute.

Add the dry ingredients to the butter and sugar mixture and gently mix through – if using a stand mixer, keep on a low speed – until the mixture comes together to form a dough.

Lightly dust the work surface with flour, tip the dough onto the surface and, using a floured rolling pin, roll it out to around 4–5mm (¼in) thick. Use a 6cm (2½in) round cutter to stamp out 15–18 rounds, rerolling to get the most out of the dough.

Place on 2 baking trays lined with baking parchment. Bake in the preheated oven for around 15 minutes or until golden brown. Transfer to a wire rack to cool.

Once the biscuits have cooled, melt the white chocolate in a small bowl over a pan of gently simmering water. Melt the dark chocolate, either in the same way or in the microwave, in bursts of around 30 seconds, gently stirring after each interval, until the chocolate has melted. Don't overheat or the chocolate will seize.

Once the two chocolates have melted, remove from the heat. Transfer the dark chocolate to a small piping bag fitted with a no. 2 round nozzle or thereabouts – if you don't have a nozzle, just snip the end of the piping bag to create a small hole.

Use a palette knife to spread a thin layer of white chocolate over the base of a biscuit, then pipe 3 thin, straight parallel lines of dark chocolate over the white chocolate layer. Turn the biscuit 90 degrees and gently drag a skewer through it up and down 3 times to create a feathered design. Repeat for the remaining biscuits. If the melted chocolate starts to set before you have finished piping, gently reheat.

Baking for Concentration

I have referred to sourdough as 'simple' in the title... that's a lie...in part. I debated including a sourdough recipe in this book – I worried that there was too much complexity to it, and frankly there can be if you let Google baffle you, but then it struck me that, firstly, learning how to bake sourdough has been one of my most rewarding baking endeavours, and secondly, you have to start somewhere with a bake, and so this can be just that: your first foray into the complex world of sourdough. Finally, it obviously tastes great and also has some health benefits such as easier digestibility, increased vitamin availability and better blood-sugar control, all of which make me even more convinced that it is worth the effort.

Sourdough is a type of bread that doesn't require commercial yeast to rise. Instead it uses a 'starter' or 'levain' – a mixture of fermented flour and water that comprises bacteria and wild yeast. This also produces the tangy flavour, chewy texture and distinctive open crumb that sourdough is celebrated for. The acidity in a sourdough loaf increases its shelf life, meanwhile the lack of commercial yeast means it doesn't contain any additives.

The first sourdough loaves I baked were not fab, and I'm still very much learning, but if you get the bug for sourdough, you really will become addicted to every aspect of the process – including the failures. The biggest lesson I have learned is that it takes practice, and some of that can only be guided by you and your little microbial ecosystem at home – you have to feel your way a bit. Research and read…but not too much. There is a wealth of info out there which is great, but it can be incredibly overwhelming and enough to put anyone off – just absorb as much of the science and technicalities as suit you. I would reckon that some of the most proficient bakers haven't understood the ins and outs of the science but instead have had an intuition and feel that have guided them – it comes back to the fact that we are all unique and can approach projects from completely different angles. Nine times out of ten, what you produce (in loaf form) will be more than edible, so please don't ditch it because it doesn't look Instagram-worthy.

The reason for sourdough's complexity is that it is very sensitive to change – vaguely reminiscent of myself. I was dubious about just how sensitive it was when I set about my sourdough mission, but quickly learned that, yes, it is… dough temperature, water temperature, ambient temperature, maturity of starter, hydration percentage, over/under proofing, inadequate shaping…THEY.ALL. COUNT.

Now this book isn't by any means an encyclopaedia of the intricacies of sourdough; I really am not experienced enough to be able to relay that sort of information. However, I want to share with you what I have learned in the hope that it can encourage you to have a go too.

I have touched on this already, but there aren't many things that can switch off my brain to the constant chatter; exercise is usually a great tonic for me but, even then, my brain whirrs. When baking sourdough, however, the concentration and focus required means I can't think of anything else. I'm the parent of a starter – essentially a child, right? – I have to judge when it's hungry and well fed, I have to time-keep, handle my dough with care, be patient, and then hope that my efforts yield successful offspring. I really can't think of anything else. Call me obsessed (I probably am) but, personally, it's magic, both literally and for my head.

As much as it may seem terribly daunting and open to pitfalls, it is 100 per cent achievable, and if all I do is pass on to you the same bug for sourdough baking that I have, such that you can become a much more proficient sourdough wizard than me, that's all that matters. Truly, the focus, concentration and mental distraction that this can provide are, in my opinion, profound and should be experienced by everyone.

So, without further ado…let's get started. Fairly intuitively, we begin with the starter. This is the living, 'breathing' being that brings your loaf to life (technical terminology), so here goes.

'Simple' Sourdough

INGREDIENTS
Strong white bread flour
Strong wholemeal bread
  flour

EQUIPMENT
Jar with a loose-fitting lid
Thermometer (if possible)
Digital scales
Spoon or spatula
A name for your starter –
  optional!

SCHEDULE

Day 1
Take your jar, and add 25g (1oz) each of strong white bread flour and strong wholemeal bread flour, followed by 50g (2oz) water heated to approximately 25°C (77°F). Thoroughly mix together and use the spoon or spatula to scrape down the sides of the jar so that it's all combined in one mass. Place the lid on loosely so that it can breathe a bit and place in a mild spot of around 20°C (68°F) for 24 hours. You can also secure an elastic band around the jar and align it with the top level of the mixture – this can help you gauge its activity.

FACT: The inclusion of wholemeal flour in the starter is useful in expediting the fermentation process as it contains more nutrients than white bread flour.

Day 2

Repeat the above process by adding (or feeding) another 25g (1oz) white bread flour, 25g (1oz) wholemeal bread flour and 50g (2oz) water heated to approximately 25°C (77°F). Return to the same mild place for 24 hours.

Baker's notes

- Your starter should be fed at approximately the same time daily. I work on an 8am or 9am schedule based on when I get up in the morning. It can alternatively be kept in the fridge to slow down fermentation, and fed much less frequently – as little as weekly. A refrigerated starter can be 'revived' after as long as a couple of weeks without a feeding.

- If your starter has been stored in the fridge, give it a couple of feeds – spaced 24 hours apart – prior to preparing a loaf.

Day 3
Now, you need to remove and discard all but 25g (1oz) of your starter before feeding once more with the same quantities: 25g (1oz) white bread flour, 25g (1oz) wholemeal bread flour and 50g (2oz) water heated to approximately 25°C (77°F).

Days 4–7
Repeat Day 3, making sure to feed your starter at the same time each day. If the ambient environment is cool (during winter months, for example) fermentation may take a little longer, so be patient. You should at some point, around Day 7 but up to Day 10, see a marked change in the activity of the starter – it should go from being dispersed with a few bubbles to rising noticeably up the jar (as much as doubling in volume) and becoming more aerated with multiple bubbles. At this point it is ready to use.

Baker's notes
- Once your starter is ready to use (from Day 7–10 onwards), 'Discard' can be used for other recipes – see Shifting the Focus, page 76 and Sourdough Discard Pancakes, pages 77–9 – so don't throw it away.

- For accuracy, most bakers weigh liquid as well as dry ingredients when making sourdough.

The Loaf

Makes 1 round loaf

Hands on time: approximately 30 minutes spaced over 24 hours
Cooking time: 45–50 minutes

INGREDIENTS

280g (9½oz) water, heated to approximately 25°C (77°F)

85g (3¼oz) sourdough starter

350g (11½oz) strong white bread flour, plus extra for dusting

40g (1½oz) strong wholemeal bread flour

10g (½oz) spelt flour (or you can omit the spelt flour and use a total of 50g/2oz strong wholemeal bread flour)

8g (¼oz) sea salt

Rice flour, for dusting proving basket or banneton

EQUIPMENT

Bowl

Digital scales

Thermometer

Dough scraper

Proving basket or banneton (or medium-sized bowl lined with a tea towel)

Dutch oven or casserole dish

METHOD

It's finally bread time...here goes.

The Starter

First off, we have to prepare the starter for action.

The starter needs to be 'mature' to work most effectively – that is, around 12 hours since its last feed – so, do this step at about 9pm the night before you wish to get cracking on your loaf, assuming you start about 9am the next day. Discard all but 25g (1oz) of starter from your jar, feed with 25g (1oz) wholemeal bread flour, 25g (1oz) white bread flour and 50g (2oz) water heated to approximately 25°C (77°F), mix thoroughly to combine. Leave to ferment overnight.

Autolyse

I used to think this step was unnecessary – why would I need to wait another 30–40 minutes? Turns out it's pretty useful. Some people only mix the flour and water at this stage – I include the starter too. The purpose of this process is to fully hydrate the flour; it increases enzymatic activity and makes the dough more extensible – essentially, stretchy and easier to work with!

Once your starter is looking active, that is, when there are bubbles throughout the mixture, it is a little frothy on top and it has approximately doubled in volume, prepare the dough. Add all but 10g (1 dessertspoon) of the 280g (9½oz) warm water to a large bowl, followed by 85g

(3¼oz) of starter. Finally add the flours and combine with your hand or a spatula to form a shaggy wet dough – yes, it's sticky, just go with it. Put in a warm place – approximately 25°C (77°F) – to autolyse for around 30–40 minutes (see Baker's notes below). NB: don't forget to feed the remaining starter left in your jar for future use.

After the autolyse, sprinkle the salt over the dough, then pour over the remaining 10g (1 dessertspoon) water – this helps to dissolve the salt. To incorporate, you now need to squeeze the dough, dimple, prod and repeatedly fold it in on itself. This seems weird and takes a few minutes to come back and resemble something of a dough, but be patient. After about 5 minutes it should form a cohesive mass again, at which point you are ready and set for the first stage of fermentation. Pop it in a clean glass bowl or plastic container with enough room for it to rise a bit. Note the time and place back in the warm environment covered with a clean damp tea towel.

Baker's notes
An ambient temperature of approximately 24–26°C (75–79°F) for autolyse and fermentation is optimal. Achieving this in cooler climates can be a bit tricky but a couple of options are to place your dough in its bowl in the oven with JUST the light switched on (check the temperature of the oven periodically with your thermometer as it can creep up) or in an airing cupboard, again monitoring the temperature.

Bulk Fermentation

This is the initial rise of the bread. During this time, fermentation continues in the dough as bacteria and yeast from the starter begin to generate organic acids and alcohol. This is where the 'strength' of the dough is going to be developed – think Popeye.

In this period, all you need to do is 'stretch and fold' the dough a series of times, keeping it in the bowl for the duration. This technique is the equivalent of kneading the dough but requires less effort and time.

Thirty minutes after incorporating the salt, you perform your first stretch and fold: wet one hand a little and scoop it underneath the dough, lifting it up, stretching it and folding it over itself. This must be performed at the equivalent of north, east, south and west of the dough. This is your first in a series of stretch and folds. You must complete this process another 3 times, spaced 30 minutes apart, returning the dough to the warm place each time. After the final stretch and fold, leave the dough once more in that warm place, covered with a clean tea towel and just wait. I work on around 1–1½ hours – you are looking for a slight increase in volume of the dough, a few bubbles will appear and it will seem billowy.

Bench Rest

Next, lightly dust your work surface with flour, then gently ease the dough from the sides of the bowl a little without deflating it. Turn the bowl over and allow gravity to take over as the dough eases itself out onto the work surface. Dust your hands with flour and gently fold the dough in on itself from each side, starting at the bottom, then left, right and top so you have a parcel effect. It can still be a little sticky at this point, but avoid adding too much flour. Use your hand and a dough scraper and flip the dough over. Upturn the bowl and place over the dough and allow it to relax for 20 minutes.

Shape

OK, so this is notoriously tricky, but you're up to it!

While the dough is relaxing, prepare your proving basket, banneton or a bowl. Liberally dust the basket or banneton with rice flour. If using a bowl, line with a clean tea towel before liberally dusting with rice flour.

To perform the final shaping, lightly dust the top of the dough with flour, then use your dough scraper and one hand under the dough to assuredly flip the dough over so that the floured side is now on the work surface.

WHY RICE FLOUR?
It won't be absorbed into the dough and helps it release from the basket or bowl the next day.

Gently lift and stretch the bottom of the dough up and over towards the middle. Next, stretch the left side over towards the centre, followed by stretching the right side out and folding over the previous fold. Finally, fold the top edge of the dough down and pinch it in place with your fingers. Now flip the dough over once more so that the seams are on the work surface. Use both hands and, keeping them in contact with the surface, cup the dough from the side furthest away from you and drag it towards you gently, rotate and drag again, then repeat. This process creates tension in the dough. Repeat a few times until the dough seems suitably taut – don't overdo it as it can tear. Once shaped, carefully lift the dough and turn it into the proving basket or bowl so that the top of the dough is face down in the bowl and the seams produced by shaping are on top. Cover loosely with clingfilm or a clean shower cap.

Final Proof
Leave your dough for a further 30 minutes at room temperature before transferring to the fridge for its long final prove overnight.

Bake
The following morning, at about 7 or 8am, place a casserole dish or Dutch oven in the oven to preheat and whack up the temperature high – I set mine at 250°C (230°C fan/500°F/Gas Mark 9) – for around 20–30 minutes (see Recipe tips, page 72).

Once the casserole dish or Dutch oven is ready, gently turn your dough out onto a piece of baking parchment larger than the loaf's circumference. Score with a very sharp knife, razor blade or lame (see Recipe tips, page 72).

Speed and depth are important here: draw the blade, held perpendicular to the work surface, quickly through the centre of the dough approximately 1–2cm (½–¾in) deep. Carefully remove the preheated dish or Dutch oven from the oven, take the lid off and, using the excess baking parchment, gently pick up the loaf and plop it in the dish or Dutch oven. Replace the lid and return to the oven.

Recipe tips

- Scoring the dough controls its rise in the oven; while not always considered essential, it is beneficial for optimum results.

- A Dutch oven or casserole dish to bake your loaf gives it the excellent crust – it's by far the best way to bake a sourdough loaf. If you only have a baking tray, preheat the tray for up to 1 hour, turn the dough out onto parchment as above, score and transfer to the preheated baking tray before returning to the oven to bake. In this instance, it's also helpful to place a roasting tray in the bottom of the oven filled with a little water to generate steam and create a nice crust and improved oven spring (the final rising that occurs when the dough goes into the oven).

Bake for 30 minutes before removing the lid and baking for a further 15–20 minutes, lowering the temperature to 230°C (210°C fan/450°F/Gas Mark 8). The loaf should be dark once baked – don't be afraid of a dark and well-baked loaf. Remove from the oven and cool on a wire rack, Don't be tempted to cut into it until it's fully cooled which can take a couple of hours.

* Freeze leftover sourdough bread on the day of baking (either sliced or as half or full loaves) to defrost and enjoy when you fancy it next.

* If your sourdough is past its best and pretty stale, it still has endless uses – don't chuck it. Make croutons for salads and soup, breadcrumbs (which can be frozen for future use), panzanella – a wonderful Tuscan salad, French toast or even bread and butter pudding (see pages 39–40)!

Shifting the Focus

Sometimes I can get really caught up in myself
– pretty selfishly so. I don't do it on purpose, but I can
become so preoccupied with minutiae that everything else
becomes irrelevant. I then perpetuate the problem by
chastising myself for feeling like this, and so I spiral into an
abyss of self-loathing. I used to find myself stuck in these
ruts for lengthy periods, but more recently I have
acknowledged the power of shifting my focus to
something else; admittedly this is easier said than done
but, like everything, practice makes perfect.

'Cognitive shifting' is something used practically in
therapy settings. It refers to identifying and accepting the
negative attitude or thought and then redirecting
attention away from the negative fixation towards a
chosen aim or goal that is more positive. For me, the
process isn't quite as prescriptive as this; instead, it's all
quite organic: I'll be hopelessly fretting over the number
of emails I have to reply to and tasks that need
completing, when I'll instinctively get up, walk out on
that part of life, wander into the kitchen and set about
baking something, more often than not using up food

that is lurking in the backs of the cupboards or the fridge. My focus will completely shift and I'll end up feeling virtuous and with improved perspective and clarity as a result of my endeavour.

Food waste poses a huge issue in today's society. Global food loss and waste reportedly contribute to around one-third of all food produced, which is staggering. This squandering of food, as well as other resources used in food production, is a major factor in the impact of agriculture on climate change.

I'm far from exemplary in my culinary practices. However, with increased awareness and understanding of the problem, I have become really passionate about minimizing food waste while maximizing reward. Besides helping the environment, the focus of using up leftover food can become an incredibly positive one and an excellent tool in shifting your brain away from negativity. Baking with this mindset can be hugely invigorating, creative and inspiring. It can teach us about food in ways we may never have previously thought possible. I swear I feel like I'm in a science lab sometimes when I start mixing my 'potions' in the kitchen.

These recipes are my staples; the ones I make most regularly, but there is a wealth of other options out there to try. Chuck sourdough discard in:

- **Granola** – it makes for incredible clusters of oaty, nutty goodness.

- **Brownies, banana bread, muffins, courgette cake** – the starter discard brings a wonderful tangy magic to the party.

- **Waffles, crumpets, cornbread, flatbreads** (see pages 24–9) – it gives these bakes a wonderful flavour and better aeration than yeasty alternatives.

- **Pasta** – yes, even pasta can be made using your discarded sourdough starter and with very pleasing results.

Use your imagination, get creative, research, focus on the goal of reducing waste – the world really is your oyster when you open your eyes and mind to the endless possibilities out there.

Sourdough Discard Pancakes

Makes
10–12 pancakes

Hands on time: 30 minutes +
30 minutes resting time
Cooking time: 20 minutes

INGREDIENTS
100g (3½oz) self-raising
  flour, sifted
20g (¾oz) caster sugar
½ teaspoon bicarbonate of
  soda
½ teaspoon baking powder
1 large egg
125ml (4fl oz) whole milk
½ teaspoon vanilla bean
  paste
115g (3¾oz) sourdough
  starter discard
15g (½oz) butter, melted,
  plus extra for frying

Blueberries and Tahini
Coconut Yogurt Topping
(optional)
120g (3¾oz) frozen
  blueberries
150g (5oz) coconut yoghurt

10ml (1 dessertspoon)
  maple syrup
20g (¾oz) light tahini

Raspberry, Peach and
Almond Cream Topping
(optional)
150g (50oz) coconut yogurt
10ml (1 dessertspoon)
  maple syrup
25g (1oz) almond butter
90g (3¾oz) fresh or frozen
  raspberries
1 peach

METHOD

For the pancakes, combine the flour, sugar,
bicarbonate of soda and baking powder in a large bowl
and lightly whisk to combine. In a separate bowl, lightly
whisk the egg before adding the milk, vanilla and
sourdough starter discard. Add the flour mixture to
the wet ingredients and whisk thoroughly to combine.
Finally whisk in the butter and leave to rest for around
30 minutes.

Lightly grease a frying pan with butter and place over
a medium–high heat. Once hot, add 2 tablespoons of the
batter for each pancake – you should fit a few pancakes in
the pan at once. Fry for around 2–3 minutes or until

bubbles appear on the top of the pancakes, before flipping and cooking for a final 2 minutes. Set aside on a cooling rack covered with a clean tea towel to keep warm while you use up the remaining batter.

For the blueberry and tahini coconut yogurt topping, warm the frozen blueberries either in a small saucepan on the hob for about 5 minutes or in the microwave for approximately 1 minute or until they have broken down and are piping hot. Combine the coconut yogurt, maple syrup and tahini in a small bowl. Dollop the yogurt mixture on top of the pancakes and scatter over the warm blueberries.

For the raspberry, peach and almond cream topping, combine the coconut yoghurt, maple syrup and almond butter in a small bowl and set aside. Warm the frozen raspberries either in a small saucepan on the hob for about 5 minutes or in the microwave for approximately 1 minute or until they have broken down and are piping hot. Stone the peach and cut into thin moon shapes, pop on a griddle over a high heat for a couple of minutes on each side before serving on top of the pancakes with the raspberries and almond 'cream'.

Baking Creatively

Art, science and maths were my favourite subjects at school. At the time, this led me to the belief that I should be an architect – without any interest in the profession – so I applied to study architecture at university, only to realize (with only a week to spare) that actually this really wasn't for me!

To this day, I'm still looking for my calling in life. However, I'm now of the belief that a profession in baking may be the thing I've been waiting to find. And really it all makes sense because baking is the perfect blend of science, maths and art. I'm obsessed with the alchemy involved in taking ingredients from one form, often inedible in their 'neat' state, to something truly delectable when combined with other ingredients and heated; the whys and hows are as important to me as producing the outcome.

This inspires me to get creative and come up with my very own recipes, a focused, exciting and rewarding endeavour, particularly when you hit on something wonderful. Then there is the aesthetic creativity of course; making something look good. Much like art, I have a style; I don't do intricate, accurate and beautiful, but kind of abstract, contemporary, expressive, with a little Impressionist influence – it's a style all of my own and I love it. It reminds me of days doing art at school, sitting on the floor splashing paint around, absorbed in my own little world; focused, but not strained or tense, just at ease, momentarily carefree and completely engrossed in the project. The huge advantage with baking is that you get to eat the product afterwards too.

It turns out that I'm not alone in appreciating the creativity involved in baking. Researchers and clinicians have discovered that there is a significant connection between creative expression while cooking and overall wellbeing.[2] The measuring, preparation, smell and taste – they all require both mental and physical attention, forcing you to focus on the present moment. Indeed, baking in this sense is a near perfect example of what psychologists describe as a flow activity (see page 52).

This recipe encapsulates the concept of creative expression in that it is so versatile. Here, I have provided the layout for making eclairs – you may not think there is too much creativity to an eclair, but really there is. Comprised of multiple component parts, each one open to manipulation, thus yielding very different outcomes. I've opted for a favourite flavour combo of mine – mocha – which I hope you agree is a winner. However, I am well aware that there are other great options to be tried.

The versatility of this recipe comes in changing the shape of the choux – go for profiteroles, big or small, Paris–Brest-style rings (a ring-shaped French dessert traditionally made of choux pastry and praline cream), jumbo eclairs or mini ones. As for the cream, you can alter the flavour very easily – try chocolate orange; add booze, curd, fresh berries, or you can switch it for crème patisserie. Decoratively, you can go wild too – nuts, gold leaf, add white chocolate 'Jackson Pollock' drizzles... Or if you feel really ambitious, you could make a bunch of profiteroles and construct a very impressive croquembouche – basically a tower of profiteroles glued together with caramel. I knew architecture would come into this somehow!

I urge you to get your creative hat on and try your hand at producing your own interpretation of these little delights.

Mocha Eclairs

Makes 10–12 eclairs

Hands on time: 1 hour
Cooking time: 25–30 minutes

INGREDIENTS

Choux Pastry Dough
85g (3¼oz) plain flour
2–3 large eggs
  (approximately
  130g/4oz beaten egg,
  see Recipe tips, page 86)
60g (2½oz) unsalted butter
55ml (2fl oz) milk
65ml (2½fl oz) water
¼ teaspoon salt
5g (¼oz) caster sugar

Coffee Cream
335ml (11fl oz) double
  cream
1½ teaspoons instant
  espresso coffee powder
25g (1oz) light brown
  sugar

Chocolate Ganache
170g (6oz) dark chocolate,
  discs or roughly chopped
1 tablespoon golden syrup
20g (¾oz) butter
90ml (3¼fl oz) double
  cream

To Decorate
25g (1oz) finely chopped
  hazelnuts

METHOD

Preheat the oven to 200°C (180°C fan/400°F/Gas Mark 6). Line 2 baking trays with baking parchment or silicone mats if you have them.

Prepare the choux pastry. Sift the flour into a bowl. Crack the eggs into a separate bowl and lightly whisk together. Combine the butter, milk, water, salt and sugar in a small saucepan and heat gently until the butter melts. Once melted, increase the heat and bring to the boil. As soon as the mixture comes to the boil, remove from the heat, quickly add the flour and beat vigorously with a wooden spoon – once combined, the mixture should resemble mashed potato. Place back over a low heat for 2–3 minutes until it is glossy and cleanly leaves the sides of the pan. Remove from the heat and transfer the dough to a large mixing bowl, leaving it for 2–3 minutes for it to cool slightly. Once slightly cooled, gradually beat in the egg a little at a time – you can use a stand mixer or spatula to incorporate the eggs. Stop adding egg when the mixture looks glossy and starts to get a sheen (see Recipe tips, page 86).

Place the dough in a large piping bag fitted with a large round or open star nozzle. Hold the pastry bag at a 45-degree angle and pipe out 10–12 eclairs around 12cm (5in) in length onto the prepared baking trays – I use scissors to snip the dough out of the bag each time I reach the end of an eclair. Dip your finger in a little water and dab the end of the eclairs to flatten any rough ends.

Place the baking trays in the preheated oven and bake for 25–30 minutes or until golden brown. Open the oven door at 15 minutes for approximately 5 seconds to release a little steam. Once the eclairs are baked, turn the oven off but leave the eclairs inside for 5 minutes to dry out a little more, before removing and placing on a cooling rack. Prick the bottom of each eclair a couple of times with a skewer at the base to allow steam to escape. Set them aside to cool completely.

Meanwhile prepare the coffee cream filling and the chocolate ganache.

For the coffee cream filling, combine the cream, coffee and sugar in a large bowl. Use an electric whisk to beat to stiff peaks – don't overwhisk. Pop in a piping bag fitted with a medium-sized round nozzle (I use a no. 7). Use a knife or the end of your scissors to make 3 holes in the base of each eclair – spaced evenly along the length and big enough for the nozzle to be inserted into it.

Pipe the cream into the holes – you will feel the eclair get heavier as the cream is added – filling generously. Place back on the wire rack.

Gently toast the chopped hazelnuts in a frying pan placed over a medium–high heat. Keep an eye on them and shake the pan a couple of times to make sure they toast evenly – don't let them catch. Set aside to cool on a plate.

Next, prepare the chocolate ganache. Add the chocolate, golden syrup and butter to a bowl over a pan of simmering water. Heat until melted. Remove from the heat and stir in the cream. Allow to cool for around 5–10 minutes before dunking the top of each filled eclair into the chocolate. Place back on the wire rack. Sprinkle the top of each eclair with the toasted hazelnuts. Eat immediately if you're impatient or wait for the ganache to set and serve at room temperature or chilled (my preference).

Recipe tips

- The amount of egg required varies based on egg size – yes, even large eggs differ in size, but also it can change based on how much moisture is cooked out of the dough after the addition of the flour.

- Unfilled baked choux pastry can be frozen and stored in an airtight container for up to a month.

Manifesting Goals

Sometimes the focus of a bake is all about the outcome, be it a personal goal, a form of communication with others or an altruistic act.

Testing myself with baking – the methods, maths, proportions and techniques – is what I really enjoy. I am so desperate to learn, and even more determined to succeed, that I will practise, using tried and tested techniques, until I achieve perfection. It's obsessive, and sometimes unproductive, but even if it's only purpose is the psychological reward, that is enough for me.

While I'm usually the most demanding customer for my bakes, others are also often at the heart of what I do. I'm a chronic people-pleaser. I absolutely hate upsetting people and possess an unrealistic need to be liked by everyone. However, from a young age, I've found it a real challenge to articulate how I feel. Initially, baking for others was something I struggled with, a lack of confidence left me paralysed to share what I had baked. More recently though, I have challenged myself to be brave and share bakes with close friends, and actually, it provides an

excellent medium for me to convey how I feel. This is something that Susan Whitbourne, professor of psychological and brain sciences at the University of Massachusetts, has found to be true in her research.[3] Be it thanks, appreciation, sympathy or love, we can convey any manner of feelings all via the medium of cake...and bread and all other tasty baked delights. Baking can be a wonderful way of showing you care, without having to say a word.

Baking for others also switches the focus from any anxious thoughts to someone else, or simply to the challenge of making something new. You can plan a bake around a specific goal, someone's request or a friend's flavour preference. If your knowledge is lacking, trial a recipe first, tweak it and formulate a plan – it will become a project and a positive focus.

On the day of baking, I always get a bit nervous: there is adrenaline, I want to do it right, but it's all positive feelings – the excited butterflies you get before you go on a weekend trip with your friends or to a party. There may be some artistic element involved – particularly where cake is concerned – and then I can get lost in my imagination. When it turns out right, I'm on cloud nine, thinking, 'I DID THAT!' If not, I've learned lessons and can try again. If I'm handing over a bake to someone else, I can hope it has gone well, but I know I've tried my best regardless; there is more excitement, nerves, and sometimes when I dig deep, even some pride. Worry is now a distant memory.

I've now baked this cake three times in the last six months for friends. It's my go-to because of its relative ease of preparation and, ultimately, winning flavour combo. Fail and it will still taste great, so I thoroughly recommend you have a go and spread a bit of the baking love.

Raspberry Chocolate Layer Cake

Serves 8–10

Hands on time: 1½ hours
Cooking time: 30 minutes

INGREDIENTS

Chocolate Cake

150ml (5fl oz) boiling water
1 tablespoon espresso
  coffee powder
235g (7½oz) plain flour,
  sifted
245g (7¾oz) caster sugar
40g (1½oz) cocoa powder
¾ teaspoon bicarbonate of
  soda
100g (3½oz) dark chocolate
150g (5oz) vegetable oil
200g (7oz) buttermilk
2 large eggs, lightly
  whisked

Raspberry Filling

300g (10oz) raspberries
40g (1½oz) caster sugar
Squeeze of lemon juice

Ganache

150g (5oz) unsalted butter,
  plus extra for greasing
1½ tablespoons golden
  syrup
210g (7¼oz) dark chocolate
190ml (7½fl oz) double
  cream

To Decorate

Mixture of fresh berries,
  approximately 150–200g
  (5–7oz)
20g (¾oz) shelled
  pistachios
Chocolate chips, optional
Freeze-dried raspberries for
  sprinkling, optional

METHOD

Grease and line 3 × 15cm (6in) tins. Preheat oven to
180°C (160°C fan/350°F/Gas Mark 4). Mix the espresso
coffee powder with the boiling water and set aside to cool.

Meanwhile, in a large bowl, combine the sifted plain
flour, caster sugar, cocoa powder and bicarbonate of soda.
Finely chop the dark chocolate and add to the flour mixture,
then stir to combine.

In a large jug, whisk together the cooled coffee,
vegetable oil, buttermilk and eggs. Pour the liquid mixture
over the dry ingredients and whisk thoroughly to combine.

Distribute evenly into your 3 tins – I'm a stickler for
precision so I weigh the amount I put in each tin to make
sure they are as equal as possible.

Bake in the preheated oven for approximately
30 minutes, or until a skewer inserted into the centre
of the cakes comes out clean. Remove from the oven
and place on a wire rack to cool completely.

*While the cakes are baking, prepare the raspberry
filling.* Add the raspberries, caster sugar and lemon juice to
a large saucepan, place on a medium heat and bring to the
boil. Simmer for approximately 15 minutes or until the
mixture thickens. Pass through a sieve – this takes a bit of
time, but is worth it, I promise. The raspberry mixture needs
to be a curd consistency: smooth but relatively thick so it

doesn't ooze out of the cake. If it's a little too thin still, place back on the heat in a clean pan and simmer a little more to reduce to the desired consistency.

Prepare the ganache. Combine the butter, golden syrup and chocolate in a bowl and set over a pan of simmering water. Heat until melted. Remove from the heat, add the cream and stir to combine. Set aside to cool for 2 hours at room temperature or in the fridge for approximately 30 minutes – not too long or it will set too hard.

Once the cakes have fully cooled, use a sharp serrated knife to trim the tops off them, creating an approximately flat surface. Place the first cake layer on a cake board, gluing it down with a smear of the ganache. Spread a layer of the raspberry filling onto the first cake, leaving a slight border at the edge, followed by a layer of the ganache – be gentle when spreading the ganache as it can merge a little with the raspberry but go with it.

Place a second cake layer on top, followed by the raspberry filling and ganache, as before, then add the final layer upside down to give the cake a flat top. Spread the ganache over the top and round the sides of the cake. I tend not to be too liberal and spread a fairly thin layer, but it's up to you how chocolatey you want it. Neaten with a cake scraper before decorating on top with the fresh mixed berries, pistachios, chocolate chips and freeze-dried raspberries, if you have them. I like to arrange the toppings in an asymmetric arc shape but tumbling the fruit, nuts and other decorations into the middle is equally effective. Refrigerate for around 30 minutes to firm up the ganache a little or serve immediately.

Recipe tips

- If you end up with some cake left after a day or so, it is epic heated in the microwave for about 10–20 seconds so that the ganache melts and you get a wicked melty hot chocolate pudding – DROOL!

- I've kept the proportions relatively moderate with a 15cm (6in) layer cake. For a larger cake, you can use 3 x 20cm (8in) cake tins and multiply the ingredients by 1½; bake the cakes at the same temperature but for around 28–30 minutes.

Baking
for Confidence

I find confidence such a tricky concept; too
little of it and we live in fear, seek unrealistic
perfection, and berate ourselves for not being
good enough; meanwhile too much and we
believe we are capable of taking over the
world and we may race ahead of ourselves,
pushing aside all offers of help, often with
really quite disastrous consequences.
Needless to say, it's no wonder that so many
of us struggle with hitting the sweet spot;
the Goldilocks zone of confidence, where
rational beliefs meet reality.

> *'If my mind can conceive it
> and my heart can believe it,
> then I can achieve it'*
> **Muhammad Ali**

I have struggled with self-confidence for...well, from birth I reckon. I was a timid child, clinging to Mum for assurance, worried about upsetting people, doing things wrong, not being good enough. This has continued into my adult life; it's something I struggle with daily and I believe has, on numerous occasions, held me back.

Viewing my life from the outside, people might assume I must be pretty confident to have put myself forward for challenges such as *Bake Off*. Not so. I cannot tell you how much courage, tears and family support have been needed to make it all possible. That, combined with my natural determination, is what has helped me, very occasionally, take a plunge. Even with this, at times I have still found myself hating situations that most would dream of due to crippling self-doubt and worry. In these instances, low self-confidence has really taken the joy out of opportunities that I should have been able to relish.

Despite this, I have learned over the years that there is always hope and that there are ways of lifting ourselves into a higher state of self-esteem. It's all about small steps, repetitive action and exposure to things that you find pleasure in and that are generally rewarding.

You probably know where I'm going next with this…yep, baking. The greatest boosts of confidence I have had are not those dictated by society's expectations, but the small things: baking something masterful from humble ingredients in my kitchen, the act of being kind to others and the differences I can make to other people's lives – more often than not through the medium of baked goods.

I'm happy to say that I'm not alone in my feelings. There is both anecdotal evidence (from friends to celebrities such as Nadiya Hussain and John Whaite, amateur bakers to professionals) and, more strikingly, research-based evidence to suggest that I'm not (that) unique! Studies report that participation in baking sessions can result in improved self-esteem, primarily as a result of increased concentration, coordination and confidence.[1] When we master a recipe, turn out a delicious bake or perfect a

new technique, we are learning different skills, and this can be a great boost for our self-efficacy. Not only that, when people produce a bake they can eat or give away to others, there is a huge sense of reward. Interestingly, this also addresses many of the topics of focus, skill and concentration discussed in the previous chapter.

In addition to providing a great way of boosting confidence through developing new skills and the possibility of relatively achievable – and delicious – successes, baking can also teach us the value of mistakes and reframe our reaction to so-called 'failures'. Developing this mindset is essential to increasing our resilience and confidence in all areas of life.

In the next few pages I discuss the concept of embracing the challenges of baking while reaping the ultimate confidence boost and reward; not only that, I touch on how this concept can be valuably applied to other areas of our lives. Home baking provides a safe environment with few or no external pressures or expectations. Embracing fear in the kitchen, as well as the inevitable mistakes we make along the way, will ultimately lead to a more satisfying, fulfilled and prosperous experience. Now if that doesn't convince you that having one almighty mishap in the kitchen is a good idea, then I don't know what will.

Along the same lines, I explore the need to let go of perfection, to lose the need to compare ourselves to others and invite greater opportunities into our lives. We see perfect bakes on Instagram and the displays in patisserie windows, but what we don't see are the hours of experience that it has taken for the professionals in the patisserie to produce those incredible displays, or the equipment they have to help them in producing 'perfect' bakes. Rather than chasing perfection, this should be about our journey, our lessons, our experience; and, given that we are the only judges of our bakes (or perhaps family and friends who – spoiler – always say things are nice), there is literally nothing to lose and everything to gain.

Finally, similar to life, baking is sometimes about the quick wins; it's about baby steps, the mini victories and the small perks that can lift you out of darkness and keep a flicker of a flame alive. I actually think this style of baking is most applicable to life and is fundamental when it comes to baking. Yes, we may take on big challenges that are rewarding but often the big challenges are made up of small ones along the way, and that is exactly what this section refers to.

Have a flick through the next few pages and I'm hopeful you may be inspired to take on a baking challenge of your own and thus experience even a momentary boost of confidence... plus some jolly yummy bakes.

Overcome Fear and Flow with the Universe

Fear or anxiety is something that affects us all to varying degrees; for some it's fleeting but for others it can be fairly life limiting. A heightened sense of fear is something that has really held me back over the years, particularly career-wise, but also in health settings, with travel and in social situations.

Sometimes fear is about self-preservation: we want to protect ourselves from feeling uncomfortable or from experiencing difficulty, so we instinctively fear anything that may put us in those situations. A fear of failure can prevent us from trying something new, or cripple us with indecision when faced with an endless list of options; what if we choose the wrong thing, we don't enjoy it, we waste money and time? Similarly, self-comparison can prevent us from attempting something for fear of how we will be perceived or whether we will match up to the standards of others. Finally, there is of course the fear of fear; an anticipation of how we will react to circumstances based on past experiences. Whether it is physical feelings, or a psychological response, the fear of these feelings can be worse than the issue at hand.

Fear generally stems from an anticipation of all the bad things that might happen; it can occur in many contexts but commonly focuses on things that we cannot control. We identify all the things that might go wrong, and nothing of what may go well.

So, having amassed enough anxiety and fear around the situation, we often decide that playing it safe is the best option. We stick to what we know, whether we like it or not, and continue in the same vein, with a resulting feeling of failure. Sound familiar?

In my experience, overcoming fear and gaining an ounce of self-belief are the products of accepting ourselves 'just the way we are'. I know, I hear you, where do we start? Well, it isn't easy, there isn't a switch and snapping out of it isn't a thing, but I do believe we can armour our brains by way of a little understanding and some simple exercises.

If you're reading this thinking that I face no fear and am queen of confidence then think again; I still face anxiety and fear frequently. I'm not preaching to you that life will magically become plain sailing, full of rainbows and butterflies by baking a cake. However, it may help.

I believe it's all about managing our emotions and not letting them rule us. Exposure to the things that scare us is a way of building resilience. It can be practised in any environment and applied to other areas of life. That's where baking comes in. When I started on my baking journey, I had no intention of becoming a master baker (to reiterate, I'm still not). I feared making a mess in the kitchen, going wrong, or producing something rubbish. As previously mentioned, I wouldn't present my bakes to people for fear of them thinking they were horrible and judging or laughing at me.

However, there was something about baking, the additional calm, intrigue, focus and creativity, that kept drawing me in. I would fail often, I'd get stressed, I still do, and yet, like a drug, I'm addicted to having another go. You see, change in any situation requires action, so in order to get better at baking – for me to learn, adapt and grow in my own little kitchen – I had to do something; knowledge and proficiency weren't going to appear on my lap without effort. I had to face my fears and see where they took me. Sometimes fear made me shake with nerves – piling cakes on top of each other was (and still is) scary business, as was shaping bread; but once I understood that when it went wrong, the consequence wasn't that bad – it still tasted OK, I wasn't a lesser human being as a result and I had learned something – I was more prepared to try again. Consistency then bred results, positive habits manifested and sometimes there was success, which for a sweet second gave me a proud and confident glow.

Now I get it, sometimes tasks seem too mammoth...like baking this chocolate-pecan babka! With a relatively complex recipe such as this, there seems to be a lot of risk. However, a task broken down into chunks becomes less daunting: firstly, you have the dough to make, then the filling to prepare, next the shaping, the proving, and finally the baking. At each step, you can learn something – if it goes wrong you can adapt it and probably save it, albeit in a slightly different form. It's a case of not rushing the process but instead trusting it, trusting ourselves.

Ultimately, we need to accept that problems won't improve through us worrying about them. Anxiety-based assumptions disempower, but replacing them with a faith that we will, one day, triumph urges us to keep striving and to continue to explore the endless possibilities out there. So, I don't know what you are waiting for: go get your apron on, make some magic and, once you've mastered the kitchen, let this mindset feed into the other areas of your life too!

Chocolate-pecan Babka

Makes 1 Loaf (serves approximately 8–10)	**Hands on time: 40 minutes + approximately 14 hours proving and resting time** **Cooking time: 25–30 minutes**

INGREDIENTS

Dough

120ml (4fl oz) whole milk

225g (7½oz) white bread flour

50g (2oz) plain flour, plus extra for dusting

20g (¾oz) caster sugar

4g (¼oz) sea salt

4g (¼oz) fast-action dried yeast

1 large egg, lightly beaten

25g (1oz) softened unsalted butter

Filling

50g (2oz) unsalted butter

50g (2oz) dark chocolate

25g (1oz) light brown sugar

½ teaspoon ground cardamom

12g (½oz) cocoa powder

40g (1½oz) pecan nuts

Cardamom Sugar Syrup

50g (2oz) caster sugar

50ml (2fl oz) water

¼ teaspoon ground cardamom

½ teaspoon vanilla extract

METHOD

Prepare the dough. Put the milk in the microwave for 20 seconds or pour into a small saucepan placed over a low heat for a minute or two – it should just be lukewarm.

Combine the flours and sugar in the bowl of a stand mixer. Add the salt on one side of the bowl and the yeast on the other. Make a well in the centre and add the milk and beaten egg. Mix on medium speed for around 5–8 minutes. Alternatively, if mixing by hand, knead the mixture for 10–12 minutes (see Recipe tips, page 107).

Add the butter and mix for a further 5–8 minutes or until it's elastic, smooth and no longer sticking to the bowl. If mixing by hand, incorporate the butter and knead for a further 10–15 minutes. Transfer to a lightly oiled bowl and cover with clingfilm. Leave for 15 minutes before transferring to the fridge to prove overnight.

The following morning, first prepare the filling. Combine the butter, chocolate, sugar, cardamom and cocoa powder in a bowl and place over a pan of gently simmering water. Heat until melted and fully combined. Set aside for around 20–30 minutes to cool and thicken.

Meanwhile, toast the pecans in a dry frying pan over a medium–high heat until slightly golden. Once toasted, allow to cool and finely chop.

Lightly grease and line a 2lb (1kg) loaf tin (measuring approximately 21 × 11cm/8 x 4½in) with baking parchment.

Remove the dough from the fridge. Roll out on a lightly floured surface to a rectangle around 30 x 40cm (12 × 16in). Spread the chocolate mixture over the dough, leaving a 1cm (½in) border around the outside, before sprinkling over the chopped pecans. Roll the dough up, starting from the longest edge, into a tight spiral. Sparingly trim the untidy ends (and no wasting them – bake those little beauties later too, be mindful as they won't need as long to bake). Take a very sharp knife and carefully cut lengthways down the centre of the dough – you will end up with 2 long hemispheres of dough, with their centres exposed.

With the cut sides facing upwards, place 1 dough length over the other to form an X, then braid together the 2 pieces of dough, ensuring the exposed filling remains upwards the whole time. Gently pick the dough up and transfer to the prepared loaf tin. Cover with greased clingfilm and leave to rise in a warm environment for around 1½ –2 hours or until doubled in size.

Around 20 minutes before you intend to bake the babka, preheat the oven to 190°C (170°C fan/375°F/ Gas Mark 5).

Remove the clingfilm from the dough and bake in the preheated oven for 25–30 minutes or until golden brown on top – the chocolate tends to make the loaf appear darker than it actually is.

While the babka bakes, prepare the sugar syrup. Combine the sugar, water, cardamom and vanilla in a small pan set over a low heat. Once the sugar has dissolved, bring to a simmer. Simmer for around 5 minutes before removing from the heat and setting aside to cool.

Once the babka has baked, remove from the oven. Brush liberally with the sugar syrup – you may not need all of it but make sure it is nicely coated. Remove the loaf from the tin and set aside to cool on a wire rack completely before cutting into it.

Recipe tips

- This dough is extremely sticky and, while it is possible to knead any dough by hand, using a stand mixer makes this bake a whole lot easier.

- Not sure whether your babka is baked? Enriched doughs, such as babka – those that contain fat, sugar and dairy – are fully baked when they reach an internal temperature of approximately 85°C (185°F), measured on a digital thermometer. Bread dough containing just water, flour, salt and yeast, reaches a slighter higher internal temperature – in the region of 90–95°C (194–203°F) – when baked. For these loaves, I tend to just tap them on the bottom. If the loaf sounds hollow, you can be fairly confident it's baked.

Embracing Mistakes

Mistakes equal failure, incompetence, stupidity, lack of self-worth, a belief that all future attempts at the same endeavour will end similarly. Sound familiar? It's certainly the view I have taken in the past. From athletics competitions to school exams, university assignments, relationships, work, even baking; mistakes were a bad thing, I shouldn't make them and if I did, I was useless!

Until quite recently, I have allowed such thoughts to pervade my brain, making me feel wholly inadequate. However, through baking, and particularly my experience on *Bake Off*, I started to develop a very different view of mistakes. You see, every time we succeed, we marvel at our brilliance and pat ourselves on the back, but what do we learn? Very little! It's only when we experience a glitch or, frankly, a catastrophic disaster that we are given the opportunity to learn from our experiences. Failures represent the biggest opportunity to progress. If I told you just how many things go wrong when I bake, you would laugh. From split caramels to curdled cake batters, seized chocolate and any manner of dough-related disasters, I have them. My *Bake Off* journey was a catalogue of ignorance, mistakes and learning that, ironically, determined my success and instilled a little confidence.

I guess this realization, in the context of baking, has helped me apply the same logic to other life situations. Don't get me wrong, I hate making mistakes, but instead of utterly cursing myself and subsequently avoiding the matter going forward, I try to open my mind to the lessons I can take from a situation (after a quick cry, of course, because I'm human and tears help me let out my frustration).

Now as far as this recipe goes, I need to start by telling you JUST how much of a disaster it was developing it – I'm telling you because I want you to realize that mistakes are real life, they happen to everyone; it's all about how we perceive them and thus react to them. Originally, I wanted to make a traditional pavlova, but around 20 eggs later and after much head scratching, I came up with a better concept, one that was a little more reliable and, in my mind, yielded a superior end product – it also happens to be quicker to make and, despite the fact that I have told you to slow down and be mindful while you bake, there are exceptions!

With every less than perfect attempt at a meringue, I learned something new: the speed of whisking, the temperature of the egg whites, adding the sugar slowly, oven temperature, and so on. The lessons I learned inspired the adaptations I made to my initial idea and the decision to opt for a much shallower meringue, with a shorter cooking time, rolled up roulade-style. I then stuffed it with the white chocolate, cream cheese and raspberry filling I had planned, and sprinkled it with some extra sparkle in the form of pistachio brittle. The recipe is still open to risks, but having been there, done that, got the t-shirt, I can assure you that there is no failure. Your meringue overbakes, it cracks and falls apart: tell me a better use for it than the most delectable dessert on earth – Eton mess. Simply crush the meringue and serve it with the same accompaniments. Seriously – the stuff is heavenly! I'm actually imploring you to make this mistake just so you can experience it.

The moral of this story?
Embrace every mistake you make from this point forward; our mistakes don't define us, it's the way we respond to them that matters. Let past experiences inform future ambitions; it sounds ever so clichéd, but have a little laugh (even cry), then learn, develop, adapt and grow.

Rolled Raspberry 'n' White Choc Pavlova

Serves 8–10

Hands on time: 40 minutes
Cooking time: 25 minutes

INGREDIENTS

Pistachio Meringue
4 egg whites, at room
   temperature
   (approximately
   140–150g/5oz)
220g (7½oz) caster sugar
1½ teaspoons cornflour
1½ teaspoons white wine
   vinegar
25g (1oz) pistachios, finely
   chopped

White Chocolate Cream Cheese Filling
130g (4½oz) white
   chocolate
50g (2oz) softened unsalted
   butter
185g (6¼oz) cream cheese,
   at room temperature
180ml (6fl oz) pouring
   double cream, at room
   temperature

Pistachio Brittle
20ml (1fl oz) water
60g (2½oz) caster sugar
5g (¼oz) unsalted butter
20g (¾oz) pistachios,
   roasted and roughly
   chopped

To Decorate
200g (7oz) fresh
   raspberries, halved and
   6–7 whole raspberries
   reserved
75ml (3fl oz) pouring
   double cream
Mint leaves

METHOD

Preheat the oven to 200°C (180°C fan /400°F/Gas Mark 6). Grease and line a swiss roll tin (approximately 23 x 33cm/9 × 13in) with baking parchment.

Prepare the meringue (see Recipe tips, page 114). Add the egg whites to a large bowl and whisk with a stand mixer or electric whisk on medium speed to soft peaks. Continue to whisk while gradually adding the caster sugar 1 tablespoonful at a time. Once all of the sugar has been incorporated, continue to whisk on medium–high until the sugar has dissolved and the mixture is smooth, glossy and forms very stiff peaks – around 5 minutes. Reduce the speed of the mixer, add the cornflour and vinegar and increase the speed for a further 60 seconds. Once mixed through, spoon the mixture into the prepared tin and gently spread evenly to the edges using a palette knife. Scatter over the chopped pistachios.

Bake in the preheated oven for 8 minutes, then lower the temperature to 160°C (140°C fan/325°F/Gas Mark 3) and bake for a further 15 minutes or until lightly browned and firm to the touch. Remove from the oven and carefully turn out onto a piece of baking parchment. Gently remove the baking parchment that was lining the tin. Set aside to cool completely.

Meanwhile, prepare the brittle. Grease a heatproof spatula. Line a baking sheet with baking parchment. Measure out the water into a small saucepan. Sprinkle over the caster sugar. Place over a low heat, swirling gently until the sugar dissolves, then turn up the heat to medium and allow to gently bubble and boil without stirring. As the mixture starts to turn a deep amber colour – approximately 165°C (329°F) on a sugar thermometer, be careful not to let it catch – remove from the heat. Working quickly, stir in the butter, before tipping in the roasted pistachios. Stir to coat them evenly in caramel before pouring out onto the prepared baking sheet. Gently spread to form an even layer and allow to cool.

Prepare the white chocolate cream cheese filling.
Heat the chocolate in a large bowl over a pan of barely simmering water. Once melted, remove from the heat and set aside to cool. Place the softened butter in a large bowl and beat on a high speed for a couple of minutes until smooth. Add the cream cheese in 2 stages, beating slightly between each addition until the mixture is well combined. Next pour in the cooled melted chocolate and continue to beat until smooth. Finally add the double cream and beat on a medium speed until the mixture leaves soft waves – don't overbeat. Cover the bowl with clingfilm and set aside until you are ready to assemble the pavlova.

To assemble, spread the white chocolate cream cheese mixture evenly over the cooled meringue. Scatter over the halved raspberries. With the long edge towards you, roll up the meringue using the baking parchment to help. Roll carefully onto a serving platter, with the join underneath.

Trim the two ends to tidy unfinished edges (and sample these – baker's perk!).

Whip the double cream to medium–stiff peaks. Pop in a piping bag with an open star nozzle fitted. Dot the top of the meringue with approximately 6–7 small star blobs. Decorate these with the reserved whole raspberries. Shatter the brittle by dropping it gently onto the baking sheet to create small shards. Pop a shard of the pistachio brittle between each blob of cream. Serve and enjoy!

Recipe tips

- For the meringue, make sure the eggs are at room temperature and your whisk and bowl are extremely clean and dry – wipe the bowl with lemon juice or white wine vinegar to be sure it's grease free. Even a speck of grease will make the egg whites deflate.

- Use free-range for the egg whites, where possible.

- To check whether the sugar has dissolved into the meringue mixture, rub a small amount between your fingers; the mixture shouldn't feel grainy.

- Make sure the cream cheese, butter and cream for the white chocolate cream cheese filling are all at room temperature for a smooth mixture.

Letting Go of Perfection

I can recall moments as a child when I would sense I had done something wrong, be it colouring outside the lines of a drawing, sweeping the leaves up badly when helping my grandad with the gardening or upsetting a friend. I'd be overcome with frustration and disappointment in myself, my eyes would sting, bottom lip would quiver, tears would flow, along with an outburst of emotion fuelled by frustration – how could I be so useless? I even put off walking until I knew that I could do it properly. I would apparently reject a helping hand to stand up and walk until, one Sunday evening, I thought, this is my time, my legs are up to this now, I've done my research, let's show them what I've got (my audience was Mum, Dad and a few teddies): I grabbed a book, balanced it on my head and, as if by magic, marched up and down the hallway for about half an hour until I had really proven my ability.

It goes without saying that, to avoid the intense feeling of disappointment or frustration, I would make sure everything was done perfectly. In the eyes of many, this would be considered a highly commendable attitude; however, it can all get very messy when perfectionism feeds into even the most inconsequential circumstances and things don't pan out as you expect.

Studies demonstrate that perfectionism is rapidly on the rise and worryingly so.[2] It is negatively affecting our health and undermining our potential. Ironically, making mistakes is a necessary part of learning, growing and being human; however, perfectionism inhibits this process. It can make us play it safe, repeat the same activities, the ones we know we can excel at, and eventually limit our desire to try new things for fear of failure.

It seems that societal expectation reinforces this mindset; we are raised to focus on achievement, and mistakes are often viewed adversely. This dichotomous way of thinking often causes perfectionists to catastrophize situations which in turn causes them to engage in negative behaviours as a form of self-punishment.

I wouldn't say I am now immune to perfectionism, but in the last couple of years, I have learnt to view it very differently. I believe that a lot of my progress has ensued as a result of baking. As I started to face inevitable mistakes in my kitchen, I acknowledged the potential for learning and growth. I started to let go of self-criticism and replaced it with fascination, as well as forgiveness and compassion; I then felt less stressed and freer. Let's be

honest, I still have
tantrums from time
to time; I'm a work in
progress, but nowadays
I can embrace imperfection,
and celebrate myself, flaws and
faults, entirely.

What is magical about this is
that, as soon as you free yourself of
the constant, unrealistic pursuit of
perfection, you open yourself up to endless
possibilities. Life becomes more enjoyable, you are
prepared to put yourself out there more and, gradually,
your confidence improves. You might not notice a change
in your mindset but suddenly you'll be baking a lime,
coconut and blueberry cake and forget to line the cake tin,
your blueberries sink to the bottom of the cake and you
then apply the icing when the cake is too warm so most of
it slides off… it's all a bit messy but, instead of being
overcome with frustration, you learn from your mistake, or
sometimes create something even better, it still tastes
great and you're still you, perfectly imperfect.

This cake probably won't provide *the* Instagram shot, it
might look a little rough around the edges, but therein lies
its beauty. This cake answers only to itself – the blueberries
may or may not sink to the bottom, it probably won't slice
cleanly – but it will taste delicious. And isn't that the
definition of a 'perfect' bake anyway?

Lime, Coconut and Blueberry Loaf Cake

Serves: Approximately 8–10

Hands on time: 25 minutes
Cooking time: 1 hour

INGREDIENTS

Cake
3 large eggs, lightly beaten
100g (3½oz) self-raising flour
½ teaspoon bicarbonate of soda
185g (6¼oz) caster sugar
160g (5½oz) softened unsalted butter, plus extra for greasing
100g (3½oz) ground almonds
50g (2oz) desiccated coconut
2 teaspoons lime zest (the zest of 1–2 limes, reserve the juice for the drizzle and icing)
3 tablespoons coconut cream (approximately 60g/2½oz)
150g (50oz) blueberries

Drizzle
45g (1¾oz) caster sugar
25ml (1fl oz) freshly squeezed lime juice

Icing
15–20ml (½–1fl oz) freshly squeezed lime juice
110g (3¾oz) icing sugar

METHOD

Preheat the oven to 180°C (160°C fan/350°F/Gas Mark 4). Grease a 2lb (1kg) loaf tin (measuring approximately 21 x 11cm/8 x 4½in) and line with baking parchment.

Crack the eggs into a small bowl and lightly whisk. Sift the flour into a large bowl, add the bicarbonate of soda, sugar, butter, ground almonds, desiccated coconut and the eggs. Beat with an electric mixer (I favour a free-standing type), on medium speed for around a minute or until the mixture is well combined. Add the lime zest and coconut cream and beat for a final 30 seconds or until well combined.

Spoon one-third of the batter into the prepared loaf tin, scatter one-third of blueberries over the batter in the tin, and repeat, adding another 2 layers of batter followed by blueberries. Once you have scattered over the last of the blueberries, poke them into the batter a little and gently level the top with a palette knife.

Bake for around 1 hour. If the cake starts to brown after 40 minutes or so, cover loosely with foil for the remaining cooking time. Keep your eye on it as it can become overbaked quite quickly. A skewer inserted into the cake should come out clean when it is cooked.

While the cake is cooking, prepare the drizzle. Place the sugar and lime juice in a small saucepan. Place over a low heat and stir until the sugar has dissolved. Set aside.

When the cake is baked, remove from the oven and skewer the top of the cake all over before slowly pouring the drizzle evenly over.

Leave to cool for 10 minutes in the tin before transferring to a wire rack to cool completely.

Once the cake is cool, make the icing. Combine the lime juice and icing sugar in a bowl and mix until smooth – it should be a stiff icing. Spread over the cake, gently coaxing it to the edges with a palette knife or a spoon.

Recipe tip

The cake is somewhat fragile – don't expect clean slices, but please overlook the 'perfection' of a wedge of neatly sliced cake and simply take pleasure from the wicked flavour.

Acknowledging and Appreciating Achievement

As humans we are motivated by our achievements; when we see progress, we feel a heightened sense of confidence and self-worth. Often, however, we set incredibly high standards for ourselves; we establish long-term goals or aims that require time, patience and considerable effort; we can face challenges, setbacks and may even be told by others that we won't succeed. This can leave us sapped and demoralized, even vulnerable to quitting and walking away. For this reason, I find it most beneficial to break down a task or aim into its constituent parts – less focus on the whole and more on the individual components. I can then celebrate the mini victories that pave the way to the end goal; it is the ability to acknowledge these mini victories that helps drive me on. The small wins are tiny confidence boosts and, crucially, a nudge to keep pushing towards the greater objective.

This applies to baking in so many ways...right now, I want to know everything, I wish to learn the 'whys' and 'hows',

the science and the skill, I want to produce incredible cakes and complex bakes. To achieve this, I can break down the challenge: understand some of the concepts and be rewarded by the respective elements of a bake as well as the final outcome. I also carry forward a better understanding of various different skills that can help towards the bigger picture of becoming a skilled baker with a bakery and lots of baking elves. The small wins are as much a boost of my confidence as the prospect of the end goal; each achievement represents 'keeping the dream alive' and I'm inspired to keep going.

Somewhat conversely, when we are consumed by a relentless task at work or the demands of life in general, it can be difficult to associate the daily grind with an end goal; we just feel like we are on a road to 'Nowheresville' – it's long and boring. I have experienced these moments frequently in recent years, and at times like this the smallest wins – of any variety – can be hugely beneficial in lifting my spirits. From fairy cakes to French patisserie, any baking triumph is enough to give me a huge sense of satisfaction. It may not take away the monotony of life but it sufficiently boosts my confidence and gives me better clarity, perspective and an appreciation of the present moment to return to other tasks with a renewed energy and positivity.

Let me be clear...our worth is not determined by our successes, achievements, productivity or wealth; it's about the ripples we make in the world; the people we touch and the differences we make; the dreams we chase and the memories we make. However, to create ripples and chase dreams, we have to start with ourselves, showing ourselves respect and applauding our mini victories; as soon as we can acknowledge our own importance and worth in this world, we can go about sharing it with others.

This millionaire's shortbread is all about various steps resulting in a final, awesome, outcome. There are challenges at each stage, lessons to learn and, more than likely, mistakes to make. Each element in its own right should be rewarded and when you get as far as the final result, it is every reason to dance around your kitchen in a state of baking-induced euphoria.

Espresso and Hazelnut Millionaire's Shortbread

....

Makes: 16 squares

**Hands on time: 30-40 minutes +
approximately 2 hours resting
and cooling time**

Cooking time: 30 minutes

....

INGREDIENTS

Espresso Shortbread

120g (3¾oz) softened
   unsalted butter, plus
   extra for greasing
60g (2½oz) golden caster
   sugar
5g (¼oz) instant espresso
   coffee powder
150g (5oz) plain flour
30g (1¼oz) rice flour

Hazelnut Caramel

60g (2½oz) blanched
   hazelnuts
200g (7oz) condensed milk
125g softened unsalted
   butter
40g (1½oz) golden syrup
45g (1¾oz) caster sugar
½ teaspoon sea salt

Chocolate Topping

200g (7oz) dark chocolate

METHOD

Preheat the oven to 180°C (160°C fan/350°F/Gas Mark
4). Grease and line a 20 x 20cm (8 x 8in) square tin with
baking parchment.

First make the shortbread. Put the butter, sugar,
espresso powder and both flours into a large bowl and

beat with an electric mixer or stand mixer, on a medium speed until the mixture just starts to come together to form a loose dough – don't overmix (see Recipe tips, page 126). Tip out into the prepared tin and press down to form an even layer. Transfer to the fridge for 30 minutes to rest, then prick all over with a fork and bake in the preheated oven for 25–30 minutes or until lightly golden. Remove from the oven and set aside to cool completely. Leave the oven on. Place the hazelnuts in a single layer on a baking sheet, place in the oven and toast for 10 minutes. Remove from the oven and set aside to cool, then finely chop.

Once the shortbread has cooled, scatter the hazelnuts evenly over the shortbread base. To make the caramel, combine the condensed milk, butter, golden syrup and sugar in a pan, place over a medium heat and stir constantly until the sugar has dissolved. Bring the mixture to a simmer and then reduce the heat to low and continue to stir, scraping the bottom of the pan to prevent it from catching, for 10–15 minutes or until the mixture has thickened and darkened to a golden brown. Once thickened, remove from the heat. Add the salt, stir through and pour over the shortbread base, spreading evenly with a spatula. Set aside to cool for at least 1 hour.

Finally, once the caramel is set, prepare the chocolate topping. Finely chop 50g (2oz) of the chocolate and set aside. Meanwhile, heat the remaining 150g (5oz) chocolate in a large bowl placed over a pan of simmering water, stir occasionally until melted. Remove the bowl from the heat and stir through the chopped chocolate. Stir until completely combined. Pour evenly over the caramel layer and smooth with a palette knife. Let the chocolate set before cutting into squares – you can make them as big or small as you like.

Recipe tips

- Don't overwork your shortbread: for a lovely, short, melt-in-the-mouth shortbread, handle delicately.

- Heat your knife slightly to help with the final cutting.

Variations

- If you hate coffee just omit it from the shortbread. Similarly, any kind of nut will work in the caramel or add your own touch; booze is a winner.

- Don't waste any leftover condensed milk, instead make ice cream: combine 200g (7oz) condensed milk with 300ml (½ pint) double cream, whisk to soft peaks, add 3 tablespoons freshly squeezed lemon juice and the zest of 1 large lemon (if you are partial to a dash of booze, throw in 3 tablespoons alcohol with the lemon juice – rum and brandy work well – and briefly whisk just to combine. Alcohol also acts as partial antifreeze, keeping your ice cream wonderfully scoopable!). Transfer to a freezerproof container and freeze for a minimum of 6 hours…and just like that, you have a delightful citrus ice cream. Stir through chunks of buttery biscuit cheesecake base (see pages 188–91) and you've got some magic RIGHT THERE!

Quick
Wins

Periods of stress, anxiety, depression and low self-esteem can be vast and enduring. I have often found that during these times there is very little that gives me joy and there certainly isn't an emergency button I can press to bring myself out of the darkness. Healing can be gradual and almost unnoticeable until suddenly I recognize that the darkness has lifted and the sun has risen again.

Despite the relative uncertainty of these periods, it's not just a case of sitting, waiting and wishing; we can take small actions to boost our self-esteem daily, almost like high-intensity interval training for the brain, which over time can build strength and endurance. One way I like to do this is find a quick win that I can easily achieve. I find that perpetual positive action gives me the perception of being more in control. As I gain control, anxiety lessens and my confidence improves a bit. It's not overnight, but with some persistence, building small wins into your daily routine can really help lift the darkness.

Quick wins can also help us to overcome specific challenges or difficulties we face. Whether applied to the work place, a hobby or a subject at school or university, if we encounter difficulty it can leave us utterly flummoxed, dejected and feeling, frankly, useless. However, returning in our minds to a time when things made sense and we experienced success can massively help in building some confidence before tackling the tricky bits once again. Sometimes, removing ourselves from the challenge completely and finding a separate task to go about mindfully and with quick results can give a sense of achievement, albeit relatively tiny, that allows us to go back to the original challenge with a bit more clarity and a slight boost of self-esteem.

If I ever face a mental block or major difficulty, my mum will always say: 'Do the bits that you can do first and come back to the hard tasks later'. Obviously, she's right – although don't tell her I said that! As someone who is keen to get things done and have a completed to-do list at the end of each day, it takes some real discipline to walk away from something or move onto another task. However, imagine we have a list of ten tasks and we start out and get stuck on number 2; we stew for hours and get nothing more done. Alternatively, we move on, smash through tasks 3–10 and end up with only number 2 outstanding. We now feel like we own the situation; brimming with confidence and possibly even armed with more knowledge from other tasks, we also then successfully tackle task 2 and go to sleep happy bunnies. OK, so it doesn't always work out as magically as that but the premise still stands.

As you have probably guessed, my ultimate source of quick-win relief is baking. Even as I have been sitting writing these recipes, I have had times when I get a bit lost for words – ironic coming from the girl who never shuts up – and I'll whip up a quick bake. I feel like I've achieved something – even if it's the only thing for the day, and then, usually at absurd hours of the evening or morning, I'll find my inner chatterbox again and start waffling into my computer.

Likewise, I have been keen to make every bake the best it can be. Therefore, I have tested recipes multiple times, tweaked, and tested them once more. However, there have been some bakes that have presented a few challenges and I've found myself really obsessing over them. I then realize this isn't about stress, so I make notes of where I am up to, move on to the next bake, get quicker results, feel more confident and return to the monster bake later with much more success.

This cracker of a recipe is actually stolen from my wonderful grandma Joan; what a blooming great lady she was. I never got the pleasure of baking with her, but enjoyed mountains of her spicy cheese biscuits – a firm family favourite. We joke that there is never too much spice (cayenne pepper) in these biscuits – that's a lie, there is, but start with ¼ teaspoon and amend from there to suit your taste buds. They are so simple to make and never fail to provide a decent confidence boost. The one issue you'll have? They're way too moreish so you'll need to whip up a second batch the following day.

Grandma's Spicy Cheese Biscuits

Makes: approximately 15 biscuits

Hands on time: 15 minutes

Cooking time: 20 minutes

INGREDIENTS

60g (2½oz) unsalted butter

115g (3¾oz) plain flour, plus extra for dusting

Pinch of salt

¼ teaspoon cayenne pepper

¼ teaspoon English mustard powder

85g (3¼oz) extra mature Cheddar, finely grated

1 large egg yolk, lightly beaten

METHOD

Preheat the oven to 170°C (150°C fan/350°F/Gas Mark 4). Line a baking tray with baking parchment.

Place the butter and flour in a large bowl. Rub the butter into the flour with your fingertips until the mixture resembles fine breadcrumbs. Add the salt, cayenne pepper and mustard powder, followed by the grated cheese; mix to combine. Finally add the egg yolk and lightly knead to form a dough. The mixture will be quite dry – if you are really struggling to bring it together, drizzle in a tiny dash of water but refrain if possible.

Lightly dust the work surface with flour. Roll the dough out to around 5–7mm (¼in) thick. Stamp out rounds (fluted or straight-sided) approximately 5–6cm (2–2½in) in diameter. Place on the lined baking tray. Reroll the dough until you have used it all up – the rerolled dough may be a little tougher but still just as tasty.

Bake in the preheated oven for 20 minutes or until lightly golden. Transfer to a wire rack to cool. A winning dinner-party snack.

Recipe tips

- Change the shape and
  create cheese straws:
  roll out the dough to
  5–7mm (¼in) thick
  and cut into strips
  approximately
  1 x 15cm (½ x 6in),
  bake and enjoy with dips.

- Switch up the cheese – choose hard, relatively
  strong cheeses for the best flavour. Alternatives
  I enjoy are: Comté, Parmesan or pecorino,
  manchego, Emmental, Gruyère.

- Don't let any remaining egg white go to waste:
  Before baking, brush the biscuits with a little beaten
  egg white followed by a sprinkle of sesame or
  poppy seeds for extra crunch and wonderful
  flavour. Use it for a rolled pavlova (see pages
  111–14) or a small batch of meringue nests.
  Alternatively, soak a slice of sourdough in egg white,
  salt, pepper and some grated cheese, if you fancy,
  and fry in a little butter for a wonderfully comforting
  eggy bread.

Baking for Brain Health

Food is one of the few essential things we require to exist in this world; not only that, it can bring us huge pleasure in a plethora of different capacities. What I find particularly remarkable is the power of food not only to influence our physical health but also to alter our psychological wellbeing.

> *'One cannot think well, love well, sleep
> well if one has not dined well'*
>
> Virginia Woolf

I was somewhat anxious about including this chapter in the book: I'm not a professional nutritionist and I haven't studied nutrition. However, as a result of my own difficulties and, at times, an unhealthy relationship with food, I have spent a good while immersing myself in understanding brain chemistry and the effect of baking and cooking, and thereby food, on our mental wellbeing.

As with most things, there is no one-size fits-all approach to managing psychological distress. However, the chemical make-up of the foods we consume has the potential to impact our brain chemistry, hormones and mental state. It's therefore worth paying attention to how foods make us feel and making tweaks to try to optimize the positive effects and minimize the negative ones.

To be clear, this isn't about demonizing certain foods while hailing others as the cure for all ill-health. This is about celebrating food and making it a positive, pleasurable and nurturing part of life. It's about considering our diet as an aspect of self-care, not beating ourselves up for certain food choices, and not judging our worth by the foods we eat – this isn't about restriction, elimination, 'rights' and 'wrongs', but simply about balance. Thus, it goes without saying that I believe we should all be setting some time aside each day or week to invest in baking, cooking and ultimately caring for ourselves in mind and body.

In the previous chapters I have discussed, at length, the rewards to be gained from the process of baking. Meanwhile, for some psychological illnesses, such as eating disorders, cooking and baking classes that focus on nutrition are reported for their benefits.[1] I certainly found that baking with a focus on the quality of the ingredients I was using helped to dissipate some of my fears around food. Similarly, for those suffering with depression or anxiety, baking can be a great source of self-care, and these benefits are enhanced when we believe the end product we produce is nutritionally valuable.

We can also instil some healthy habits by learning to cook and bake; for example, starting the day with a nutritious breakfast or opting for a homemade snack that hits the spot in terms of keeping our energy levels, and thus mood, more stable. Then when it comes to the eating, we can implement a little discipline for more reward: being mindful as we consume what we have made, eating without distraction, being present and reconnecting with our bodies. There is so much more to be gained mentally when we make mealtimes relaxing and enjoyable rather than fraught or with our mind elsewhere. Finally, besides the satisfaction and pleasure of the food itself, the foods we choose to consume can directly impact other activities known to assist in building a healthy brain. From fuelling exercise to improving focus and even aiding sleep, our food choices impact the potential for us to get the maximum from a number of other day-to-day endeavours.

The recipes that I've produced in this chapter aren't nutritionist-approved elixirs, they don't make false claims of bake-induced euphoria; however, they are some great-tasting, nutritionally dense options that I thoroughly recommend. I'm keen to point out that we are all wonderfully unique, and what works for one person doesn't necessarily work for everyone. Therefore, I encourage you to become more in tune with your own body. Use these recipes and the information provided as inspiration, allow yourself to get creative, generate some of your own ideas using my suggestions as templates, create some ingenious bakes that nourish your soul – and when you come up with something magical, don't forget to share your secrets with me!

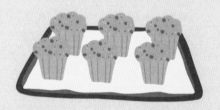

Food and
Brain Health

It's fairly well established that the foods we eat can affect our mental health. Unfortunately, the information that we are exposed to can be extremely confusing, conflicting and, at times, incredibly dangerous. As I have already mentioned, I am not medically qualified and this chapter is not intended to provide any hard and fast 'rules' about what is 'right' or 'wrong' when it comes to the foods we eat. What I can do is impart the little knowledge I have picked up over the years and demonstrate how a focus on good-quality ingredients and a positive relationship with food can bring real rewards for your mental wellbeing. I urge you to seek advice from a professional should you need it, or immerse yourself in credible, evidence-based literature if you wish to further your understanding.

I am extremely lucky to have grown up in an environment where there has always been an abundance of varied, nutritious foods on offer. I ate olives as soon as it was safe to, I'd lap up homemade lentil curries with naan bread, fish pies were a favourite, a creamy mushroom pasta dish was a weekly feature and of course there was endless fresh bread and butter. Most importantly, potato crisps and sweets were also on the menu, and I believe the lack of restriction when it came to these foods made me largely indifferent to them.

When I started to struggle with my mental health and subsequently an eating disorder, I became more and more aware of what I was eating. Initially there was denial of 'bad foods' and an obsession with 'less is more'. This led to huge mood swings, I'd cry frequently, I would have no energy, my sleep would be disturbed and I found little enjoyment in just about anything. It also, ironically, made me obsessed with sugar-laden processed foods; I was craving the very thing I now denied myself.

As I began to understand the implications of eating a nutrient-deficient diet, I became increasingly intent on learning about food and its impact on my mental health. Despite an onslaught of advice to suggest otherwise, it seems there is no one specific right way to eat; we are all unique and thus should react to our own needs and not those of our friends or internet gurus. However, the primary advice from reliable nutritionists and dietitians remains fairly consistent: eat variety; prioritize wholefoods rich in fibre, such as wholegrains, beans, legumes, nuts, fruits and veg; add herbs, spices and olive oil to meals; get in plenty of oily fish for the 'brain gains' and don't eat an excess of ultra-processed foods. Nevertheless, nothing should be off limits, food is to be enjoyed, not used as reward or punishment; it should bring us together in communities and be savoured.

Obviously, there is a whole lot more information out there but as I dipped my toe in the ocean of nutrition, I also developed a desire to get experimental in the kitchen; partly out of a need for control, but also to explore flavours, textures and variety. As I prepared foods that I knew were likely to support my physical and mental health, I felt both the therapy attributed to the process and vast improvements to my mood; more than likely as a result of better food quality and quantity. As soon as the kitchen became my playground, I noticed huge gains in my overall wellbeing.

I've always been a breakfast eater, and nowadays, I'd go as far as to say it's my favourite meal of the day. That's not to say it is the most important meal of the day – interestingly, recent evidence doesn't always back up this long-held belief – but it's my most important meal. It's a wonderful morning ritual from preparation right through to consumption.

Porridge became a staple for me at around the age of 15. I remember that it was Mum's typical breakfast and as a young child I would hang over her bowl demanding a spoonful or two. Through the darkest days of my eating disorder, porridge remained a crutch – back then it was a small portion and, with hindsight, massively lacked imagination, but over the years I have learned the endless potential of this humble meal, and it NEVER gets old. I switch up the spices and fruits I use, I always add a healthy dollop of live yogurt (a gut-friendly and thus

brain-boosting ingredient), nut butter – which I also eat out of the jar (everyone does right?) – or a sprinkle of mixed nuts or seeds.

If you follow my social media accounts, you will know just how committed to porridge I am. Thus, it had to be included in the recipe line-up here. It was a tough call deciding which flavour combo to choose but this apple pie porridge always brings me comfort; a hug in a bowl. You can, however, quite easily adapt this. Carrot cake porridge is another hero flavour choice – switch out the apple and add a handful of grated carrot. Alternatively, top with baked fruit (mentioned in my crumble recipe on page 47) or omit the spice, or use honey instead of sugar and scatter with seasonal fresh berries in the summer months. Having tried this recipe, continue to explore the endless possibilities and make porridge your morning canvas.

Spiced Apple Pie Porridge

Serves 1

Hands on time: 15 minutes
Cooking time: 15 minutes

INGREDIENTS

100g (3½oz) cored, peeled
apple (about 1 small
apple, I like Jazz or Pink
Lady), roughly cubed
10g (½oz) demerara sugar
½ teaspoon ground
cinnamon
35g (1¼oz) jumbo
porridge oats
200ml (7fl oz) milk (cows',
oat or almond)
Pinch of freshly grated
nutmeg
Pinch of salt
20g (¾oz) sultanas

Toppings

1–2 tablespoons full-fat
Greek yogurt
10g (½oz) pecan nuts,
lightly toasted

**Almond Maple Cream
(optional)**

10g (½oz) almond butter
½ teaspoon maple syrup
1–2 teaspoons milk

METHOD

First stew the apples. Combine the apples and sugar in
a small saucepan. Place over a medium heat, stirring
occasionally until the sugar has dissolved, then cook until
the apples have softened but not completely lost their
shape – approximately 5–10 minutes.

Once the apples are cooked, remove from the heat and stir through half the cinnamon. Remove half of the apples and set aside in a small bowl until later.

Add the oats, milk, remaining cinnamon, grated nutmeg, salt and half the sultanas to the saucepan. Place over a medium heat and cook for 5–7 minutes, stirring periodically until the porridge has thickened to a desired consistency.

For the optional almond maple cream, place the almond butter, maple syrup and 1 teaspoon milk in a small bowl and stir to combine. Drizzle in the extra 1 teaspoon milk if needed to achieve a loose paste.

Once cooked, transfer the porridge to a serving bowl, top with a dollop of Greek yogurt, the reserved stewed apple and remaining sultanas, drizzle over the almond maple cream, if using, and sprinkle with toasted pecans. Serve immediately.

Variation

Make the porridge as above, mix it with the toppings plus an extra drizzle of maple syrup, then transfer to a 15cm (6in) greased ovenproof dish and top with either 2 tablespoons of leftover crumble topping (see pages 44–7) or a handful of granola and bake in a preheated oven at 180°C (160°C fan/350°F/Gas Mark 4) for 25 minutes. Serve with a spoonful of yogurt.

Do What's Right For You

For those of us who face mental health challenges, the onslaught of advice, news and information on just about everything can not only be confusing but also potentially destructive. From exercise and nutrition to business and relationship advice, we can always be convinced that we should be doing better, more or something different.

Groups of unqualified 'experts' in various fields invent hard and fast 'rules' that can damage us both psychologically and physically. Ironically, those of us who struggle with mental health often like the idea of rules and are compelled to respond to them. Rules can help to direct our behaviours; without them, the responsibility is on us to trust our judgement...which we often don't.

I sometimes try to think back to when I was a young child. I explored the world with curiosity and a sense of intrigue; I behaved, thought, ate, exercised, laughed, cried instinctively. Even at such a tender age, our personalities and behaviours vary drastically – without thinking about it, as young children we naturally act in a way that best suits

our individual needs and wants. As we carry on into adulthood, our needs, preferences, and character traits continue to differ; therefore, what works for one person won't necessarily be generalized to the population at large. However, as we grow older, societal norms, external pressures and expectations begin to guide our behaviour and direct our choices. This isn't necessarily all negative, but it can mean that we fall out of sync with our own individual needs and instead try to mould ourselves to fit some received version of 'perfect' or 'normal' or 'correct', which may not work for us in reality.

Once I grasped this concept, I learned to be more attuned to the needs of my own mind and body as opposed to those of others, particularly when it comes to things I enjoy in life, what goals I pursue and how I nurture my mind and body. When I started to bake, it wasn't something that anyone in my family had pursued and it wasn't something encouraged at school; it's not necessarily hailed as a big money earner or high-flying career choice. But I found a passion for it, which made it right for me at a particular time in my life.

Similarly, when it comes to when and what I eat I've always been someone who has preferred eating little and often and, having dabbled with extended periods without food – because I read somewhere that snacking was 'bad' – I quickly learned that the benefits of snacking for me far outweighed the supposed disadvantages, so I reintroduced the snacks with huge pleasure. Phew! As it turns out, current research into the effect of snacking on our health is very much dependent on individual circumstance[3] – so I reiterate, do what works for you.

Now, I'm pretty pleased with myself that in reminding you to embrace your individuality and stop reacting to what others say is 'right' or 'wrong', I've managed to bring the subject onto snacks…and as I'm here, I'll keep going. When it comes to my regular snacks of choice, I tend to seek out things that balance some quality nutrients with great flavour. Why? Because, besides the enjoyment I get in the eating, I also like to think my body and brain will get the same pleasure. I try to prioritize ingredients high in fibre, protein, essential fats, prebiotics, probiotics, vitamins and minerals. This ensures that my snacks provide more of a sustained energy boost instead of wild ups and downs, which can exacerbate anxiety. I'm feeding my gut microbiome and thus my brain and I'm enjoying every mouthful of what I eat…what more could I ask for?

Bearing all this in mind, I have drawn on one of my favourite snacks, flapjack. Purists may argue that it shouldn't be called a flapjack, but I can assure you it tastes good. Not only that, I get the pleasure involved in baking it – I swear this is one of my favourite bakes purely due to the fact that licking the bowl and eating the 'raw' ingredients yield as much pleasure as the end product. Loaded with nuts and seeds, it's higher in protein than your standard flapjack and contains essential fats that, once broken down, can improve brain-cell communication. The dates provide a natural sweetener and along with the oats up your fibre intake for the day. I've also added a little lemon zest which, paired with the coconut, is always a winner. In my eyes, all of this information provides even greater reason to give them a try…and if you're not a snacker, well they're worth trying anyway! And of course feel free to get inventive and put your own spin on this recipe, mixing up the flavours with your own preferences to find a snack tailor-made to you.

Superhero Flapjack

Makes: 16 flapjacks	**Hands on time:** 20 minutes
	Cooking time: 25 minutes

INGREDIENTS

200g (7oz) medjool dates

200g (7oz) rolled oats

½ teaspoon sea salt

60g (2½oz) desiccated coconut

40g (1½oz) toasted flaked almonds

15g (½oz) sesame seeds

15g (½oz) pumpkin seeds

Zest of 1 lemon

100g (3½oz) unsalted butter, plus extra for greasing

80g (3oz) demerara sugar

60g (2½oz) honey

110g (3¾oz) smooth peanut butter

METHOD

Preheat the oven to 180°C (160°C fan/350°F/Gas Mark 4). Grease and line a 20cm (8in) square baking tray with baking parchment.

Cover the dates in 250ml (8fl oz) boiling water and leave to soak for 10–15 minutes. Then drain thoroughly and transfer to a food processor and blend until the mixture resembles a thick paste.

Add the oats, salt, desiccated coconut, flaked almonds, seeds and lemon zest to a large bowl and briefly mix to combine.

Combine the butter, sugar and honey in a large saucepan. Place over a low heat until the sugar has started to dissolve, the butter has melted and a warm syrupy liquid has formed. Remove from the heat and stir through the peanut butter and date paste. Mix well to combine – it should form a thick paste.

Pour the dry ingredients into the wet and stir to combine, ensuring all of the oat mixture is evenly coated.

Tip the mixture into the prepared baking tin, smoothing with the back of a spatula or a palette knife.

Bake in the preheated oven for 25 minutes or until lightly golden on top and softly set. Leave to cool in the tin before slicing into 16 portions. This flapjack has a wonderfully fudgy consistency.

Variation

Switch this up in the winter months – chuck in some ground cinnamon or mixed spice; opt for ground almonds and finely chopped toasted pecans in place of the coconut and flaked almonds; use orange zest instead of lemon, then chuck in a handful of cranberries and a sprinkle of crystallized ginger for good measure.

Gut Health

The human body is a mind-blowing machine don't you think? It astonishes me just how much it is capable of, and how much we still don't know it's doing on a daily basis. In recent years, some very clever people have unearthed even more information about its capacity; there is a growing body of research around our gut and its relationship with the brain – commonly referred to as the 'gut–brain axis'.[4]

'Gut health' refers to the functioning of our entire gastrointestinal tract from entry to exit. And it is the bacteria that live in our guts that seem to play a fundamental role in not only our physical but also our mental wellbeing. These bacteria can help us digest food, modulate immune function and reduce inflammation. Given that our brains require energy to operate optimally, it makes sense that squeezing all of the nutrients from the food we eat can help. Most incredibly, the bacteria living in our guts can go as far as making vitamins and synthesizing a number of compounds fundamental to brain function. These include short-chain fatty acids, which help in providing energy, and neurotransmitters such as serotonin, which is involved in regulating emotion.

Prebiotics and probiotics (those words we hear so often these days) are the optimal sources for the gut microbiome. Prebiotics represent foods that are fibre rich – wholegrains, veggies, fruits and legumes. Meanwhile, probiotic sources include live yogurt and fermented foods such as kimchi, sauerkraut, kefir and even some good-quality cheeses. Essentially (and probably very unscientifically put), they feed our little gut-bugs and keep them in tip-top working order.

In a similar vein, tea, coffee, cocoa powder and good-quality dark chocolate are said to possess brain-protective properties in the form of polyphenols. Polyphenols are another source of 'food' for our gut microbiome and have been shown to enhance the elasticity of blood vessels, allowing blood to flow more freely, thus enhancing working memory. As with everything, it's all about moderation. Furthermore, research on this topic is constantly evolving and, thus, should be viewed conservatively. However, I for one can provide anecdotal evidence to back up this premise; a coffee or two a day can be hugely beneficial in lifting my mood and concentrating my mind, while dark chocolate ticks all of the happiness boxes.

I realize I have gone a bit science-y here, but I feel it's relevant and pretty enlightening. This isn't about demonizing foods or shunning certain ingredients. It's simply a message that a happy gut is one of a variety of contributors to a happy brain. What I love about this information though is that not only is the act of baking a source of therapy, but the ingredients we use in our bakes can also, seemingly, upgrade our brain health.

Formulating a bake containing all of these gut-healthy ingredients while still being palatable was rather tricky, but I'm never prepared to compromise on enjoyment factor when it comes to a bake. However, I seem to have mashed a heap of gut-friendly nutrients into these little muffins and still created something quite delectable. Banana, wholemeal flour, natural yogurt, chocolate, coffee, even a dash of olive oil (another champ for the gut microbiome), cinnamon and a handful of pecans, they have it all going for them. A perfect on-the-go snack or anytime pick-me-up.

Chunky Monkey Muffins

Makes: 10   **Hands on preparation: 20 minutes**

Cooking time: 20 minutes

INGREDIENTS

55g (2oz) wholemeal flour

55g (2oz) plain flour

¼ teaspoon salt

½ teaspoon bicarbonate of soda

50g (2oz) caster sugar

50g (2oz) light brown sugar

½ teaspoon ground cinnamon

25g (1oz) cocoa powder

75g (3oz) dark chocolate chips

25g (1oz) chopped pecan nuts

1 large egg

100g (3½oz) natural yogurt

60g (2½oz) olive oil

1½ teaspoons instant espresso coffee powder, diluted in 50ml (2fl oz) boiling water and cooled

100g (3½oz) very ripe banana (approximately 1 medium banana), mashed to a purée

METHOD

Preheat the oven to 180°C (160°C fan/350°F/Gas Mark 4) and line a muffin tin with 10 paper cases.

In a large bowl, combine the flours, salt, bicarbonate of soda, caster sugar, light brown sugar, ground cinnamon, cocoa powder, chocolate chips and chopped pecans.

In a separate bowl, lightly whisk the egg before adding the yogurt, olive oil and coffee mixture. Whisk

Recipe tips

- Serve warm with yogurt. To make your own: heat 500ml (17fl oz) whole milk in a large saucepan to 85°C (185°F), measured on a digital thermometer. Once at 85° (185°F), remove from the heat and allow to cool to 46°C (115°F) – it takes a little while but don't walk too far from it. Once the milk reaches 46°C (115°F), working quickly, whisk in 2 tablespoons live active yogurt, and immediately transfer to a vacuum flask or yogurt maker. Allow to set for 8–12 hours – during this time, do not move the flask.

- These muffins stay moist because of the addition of banana, but if you want to revive them after a day or two, pop in the microwave for a 10–20-second blast; the chocolate chips will melt. It's a winner, trust me.

thoroughly to combine the ingredients. Finally whisk in the mashed banana.

Add the wet ingredients to the dry ingredients and use a wooden spoon or spatula to thoroughly combine.

Distribute the batter evenly between the muffin cases. Bake in the preheated oven for 18–20 minutes or until risen and springy to the touch.

Exercise
and Baking

Besides baking, my other passion is exercise; be it a long walk, a run, 20 minutes in the gym or a Pilates class, it never fails to lift my mood. I was always an active kid, I hated sitting still – even a PlayStation didn't grasp my attention. I was much more content racing around on my bike or on rollerblades; scrapes and bruises were permanent features but never enough to deter me. For a few years, I channelled my energy into running around an athletics track for fun; still today I seek the same exercise-induced thrill. There was a time when I allowed exercise to become tiresome and a chore; I used it as punishment and as a means of controlling my body. Fortunately, I quickly recognized the destructiveness of this mindset and have since exercised to make my head clearer, to feel stronger and happier.

It is well established that exercise of any form is one of the best things we can do to nurture our brains and bodies. As with everything, moderation is key, but broadly speaking it does us the world of good. As mentioned above, we shouldn't be driven by aesthetics but instead by the healing powers of exercise. Besides physical benefits,

exercise is reportedly one of the greatest investments we can make in our long-term brain health. From reducing the risk of depression and anxiety to improving social skills, cognitive function, sleep and even reversing brain ageing, exercising helps. Pair that with baking and you have yourself some pretty robust defence mechanisms against psychological and emotional distress.

With the above in mind, I love to conjure up bakes that support my exercising endeavours. What I find so astonishing about baking is its ability to provide comfort in so many different guises. I've already discussed at length the reward involved in the process of baking, the confidence boost it can provide and its ability to shift our focus, but getting creative with bakes that support exercise provides a double whammy. We can bake to calm the mind, feel empowered, change our mindset and fuel our exercise, which in turn has the power to restore our brain health.

Whether I am going for a run or setting off on a long walk, even on a picnic with friends, I like a nourishing energy boost. I remember back to my school days when my snack was often a slice of malt loaf; I lived for break-time because I enjoyed it so much. Nowadays, I'm pretty sure I would be considered a little unusual for my preference but I stand my ground, I love it.

Now I know this isn't a traditional yeasted malt loaf...and for that I'm sorry if I've built up your hopes only to under-deliver at the final hurdle. However, I don't think this will disappoint. Think of the moistest cake, full of ginger, a real essence of sticky toffee pudding that comes from the dates and then that wonderful malt flavour. Packed full of fruity fibre, vitamins and minerals and low in fat (although I strongly advise topping with a smear of butter or even almond butter when serving – it works, honest), this never fails to provide quality energy.

Ginger Sticky Toffee Malt Loaf

Serves: 10

Hands on time: 20 minutes
Cooking time: 1 hour

INGREDIENTS

120g (3¾oz) stoned dates

2 balls stem ginger, drained
of syrup and chopped

75ml (3fl oz) warm strongly
brewed black English
breakfast tea

25g (1oz) dark brown
muscovado sugar

20g (1oz) light brown sugar

85g (3¼oz) malt extract

30g (1¼oz) sultanas

1 large egg, lightly beaten

125g (4oz) plain flour, sifted

5g (¼oz) ground ginger

¼ teaspoon bicarbonate
of soda

½ teaspoon baking powder

Syrup glaze (optional)

1 tablespoon malt extract

1 teaspoon syrup from stem
ginger jar

METHOD

Preheat oven to 150°C (130°C fan/300°F/Gas Mark 2), then grease and line a 500g (1lb) loaf tin.

Cover the dates in boiling water and leave to soak for 10–15 minutes, then drain thoroughly. Combine the drained dates with the stem ginger and the warm tea in a food processor and blend until the mixture resembles a thick purée. Transfer to a medium bowl and mix in the sugars, malt extract, sultanas and beaten egg.

Next, add the sifted flour and ground ginger to the mixture and stir thoroughly to combine. Finally, quickly stir in the bicarbonate of soda and baking powder.

Pour into the prepared tin and bake for around 1 hour or until a skewer inserted into the cake comes out clean. Remove from the oven and leave to cool in the tin.

Recipe tip

This cake keeps for up to 5 days – it actually improves after a day or so. If I don't think I'm going to get through it all in that time, I like to freeze it in slices and grab it out in emergencies!

If using the syrup glaze, mix the malt extract and ginger syrup in a small bowl and, while the cake is still warm, brush the top with the mixture for extra stickiness!

Spread with butter and serve with a cup of tea or take on a picnic, hike or cycle ride for on-the-go fuel.

Variation

If you are not a fan of ginger, you can omit both the stem ginger balls and ground ginger. I would add an extra date or two and you can choose a different spice if you wish; a dash of ground cinnamon, mixed spice or ground cardamom would work wonderfully.

Better Sleep, Better Mind

Fairly fittingly, I am ending this chapter in my bed...not literally, but on the subject of another of my favourite pastimes: sleep. Ironically, I've always been pretty poor at sleeping. I vividly recall a motto I frequently used as a child: 'sleep is time that could be spent on much more exciting things'. Oh, how wrong I was! Nowadays, I long for the moment when I wriggle into bed at night.

Sleep represents another essential factor in protecting our brain health. For some time, it was believed that poor sleep was a symptom of mental-health problems. However, more recently, it has been established that sleep disturbance is a contributing factor in the development and maintenance of mental illnesses. Poor sleep is reported in a vast proportion of people who suffer with depression, while research demonstrates that symptoms of anxiety increase as sleep quality declines.[5] Sleep's benefits don't stop at mental-health advantages either; quality sleep protects against the onset of cognitive decline and illnesses such as dementia. Not only that, it can help with concentration, focus, learning and memory, and also helps to protect our immune systems and aid physical recovery from illness or injury. With improved concentration and focus, we are more alert and capable of engaging in day-to-day activities, be they work, baking or socializing. Similarly a rested body enjoys exercise considerably more than an exhausted one. As we now know, these factors in turn help in reducing symptoms of psychological distress. Simply put, sleep is pretty damn important!

There are a number of ways we can improve our sleep, such as by maintaining a relatively strict bedtime routine; going to bed and getting up at similar times each day; making our bedroom environment conducive to sleep – noiseless, lightless, temperate; avoiding stimulants such as alcohol and caffeine, as well as light-emitting devices; and finding calming distractions to engage in in early evening that limit the potential of getting overwhelmed by anxieties prior to bedtime. Besides these useful techniques, food can also play a part in our sleep quality. A heavy meal late in the evening can be detrimental to a

good night's sleep; similarly poor food choices can hinder sleep quality. Conversely, going to bed hungry is known to interfere with our sleep and there is some evidence to suggest that certain foods can be beneficial.

When it comes to the foods I consume for dinner and into the evening, I try not to obsess too much over it; after all, the worry won't help and satisfaction and variety are also the key to a happy, healthy mind. However, I do enjoy any excuse to concoct a sleep-inducing bake and couldn't neglect sharing my favourite evening snack with you: banana bread granola. It's also an ode to the bake that went 'viral' in 2020!

This recipe combines banana, walnuts, flaxseed and oats, among other yummy ingredients, which contain protein, fibre, healthy fats, omega-3s and omega-6s, vitamins, minerals and a pinch of melatonin, all reportedly favourable for sleep. Served with milk or a dollop of live yogurt, and topped with cherries or kiwifruit – both recognized for their sleep-inducing capabilities – and you've got a potentially unbeatable medley. It's also quick to prepare and gives your house the most wonderful smell.

Slight side note: granola (and cereal in general) was something that really aided my eating-disorder recovery. It's easy to consume, full of nutrition, and if you try making it yourself, very adaptable in regards to the ingredients used. The process of food preparation can also be really effective in facilitating treatment.

To be clear, there are a huge number of factors at play when it comes to a good night's sleep. As with so many things, it is about doing what works for you, making small changes over time to see which things help you get the Zs you need to wake up feeling refreshed. What you find beneficial doesn't need to be backed up by science, nor does it need to be what other people do; if it works for you, then run with it – figuratively of course. Regardless, if you like bananas and granola, actually even if you don't, you must try this recipe – it's such a winner.

However, if you can't face a snack after dinner, a warm milky drink is an excellent alternative. In particular, malted milk – malt powder combined with milk – has long been recognized for its sleep-inducing powers. I also love golden milk, a traditional Indian drink with reported healing properties. I can't back up the claims that suggest completely magical healing, but it tastes great and leaves me suitably dozy at night. To make it, combine 250ml (9fl oz) oat or almond milk, 12g (½oz) honey, 1 teaspoon coconut oil (optional), ½ teaspoon ground turmeric, ¼ teaspoon ground cinnamon, a pinch of ground pepper, 5g (¼oz) peeled and grated fresh ginger and 5 bashed cardamom pods in a saucepan and bring to a rolling boil. Simmer for 10 minutes, then strain and serve.

Banana Bread Granola

Makes: about 400g (13oz)/8–10 servings   **Hands on time: 10 minutes**
Cooking time: 30–40 minutes

INGREDIENTS

100g (3½oz) walnuts
50g (2oz) almonds
260g (8oz) oats (or a combination of oats and spelt or rye flakes)
1 tablespoon demerara sugar
1 tablespoon flaxseed
2 heaped teaspoons ground cinnamon
½ teaspoon sea salt
55g (2oz) coconut oil
100g (3½oz) maple syrup

120g (3¾oz) very ripe banana (approximately 1 medium banana)
30g (1¼oz) toasted flaked coconut (see Recipe tip)

Recipe tip

If your coconut flakes aren't already toasted, add them to the granola mix 5–10 minutes before the end of the cooking time.

METHOD

Preheat the oven to 160°C (140°C fan/325°F/Gas Mark 3). Line a large baking tray with baking parchment.

Roughly chop the walnuts and almonds and combine in a large bowl with the oats, sugar, flaxseed, cinnamon and salt.

Next, combine the coconut oil and maple syrup in a saucepan. Place over a low heat and stir occasionally until melted. Meanwhile mash the banana in a separate bowl.

Add the mashed banana to the melted coconut oil and maple syrup mixture; whisk thoroughly to combine.

Pour the wet ingredients over the dry ingredients and mix until the oat mixture is fully coated.

Spread onto the prepared baking tray – leave some clumps stuck together; once baked they will form wonderful clusters.

Bake in the oven for 30–35 minutes. Keep an eye on it towards the end of the baking time to prevent it from catching. Remove from the oven, add the toasted coconut flakes and allow the granola to cool on the baking tray – it will continue to crisp up.

Baking for Happiness

I'm rounding off our little baking adventure in the ultimate manner: baking happy. Some things in life are debatable but one thing I know for sure is that baking in one way or another brings pure happiness. For the person who bakes or for the people who receive the results – whether for a special occasion that is being marked or simply for afternoon tea – baking never fails to enrich our lives.

*'Life is a journey with problems to solve,
lessons to learn but most of all
experiences to enjoy'*

This book hasn't been a mission to hail baking as a
solution to life's problems, nor has it been an attempt to
convince people that it is superior to other activities,
hobbies or therapeutic interventions. I've simply wanted to
share my experience (and that of others) to highlight the
joy that can be felt via the medium of baking. Not only that,
the process of writing this book has helped me recognize
just how much we can gain from the act of baking; from
meditation, to feeding the gut (and brain – in more ways
than one) and making friends. I would like to add: baking
may not be for everyone, and if it just doesn't light up your
brain in the same way that I have described here, please
don't feel despondent or a failure. The techniques,
emotions and processes that are described within these
pages are not all limited to baking; they can be applied to
any manner of activities. It's about engaging in things that
you feel naturally drawn towards; acting on whatever excites
you, not overcomplicating matters or fearing failure, just
enjoying a process for what it is worth, to you.

In these final few pages, I hope to take you to a place of
baking euphoria, concluding our journey with some true
classics. This chapter explores the different ways that baking
can inspire happiness including the concept of baking with a
higher purpose as a path to fulfilment and that of social

eating for the importance of human connection, notably around food. I also discuss the idea of foodie traditions – the significance of a particular bake can be rooted culturally, in religion, or simply serve to remind us of happy times in our pasts.

For a long time now, my primary aim in life has been to be happy. It seems such a simple wish and yet elusive to so many of us. More often than not we are led to believe that happiness is based on external influences; people, places or things. Ultimately though, it all comes down to us; choosing empowering thoughts, making it a habit to see the positives in situations, remaining in the present, letting go of comparison, loving everything in the world and embracing what is. Baking is not necessarily the answer, but the process could assist us in embarking on a journey of growth, psychologically, spiritually and physically. As we take small steps towards establishing self-mastery, so too may we start to experience sustained happiness.

Baking
with a
Purpose

As we have now established, the benefits to be gained from baking are vast. Similar to athletes achieving world records, musical lyrics written spontaneously and effortlessly, and 'lightbulb moments' in science, there are times when everything comes together in harmony when we experience pure joy, enlightenment and success.

I have enjoyed some of my greatest bakes when the outcome is appreciated by others – a surprise bake for someone brings another level of adrenaline-fuelled excitement. Ultimately, baking with a higher purpose and shining a light on the lives of others generates the truest happiness.

In the last few years, chefs and bakers alike have pushed boundaries, exploring inventive flavour combinations and introducing us to endless tasty possibilities. While I'm always intrigued to try new things, I'm also a big fan of the classics; the ones that go back generations, bring us comfort and never fail to deliver.

The internet informs me that carrot cake is the third most popular cake in the world. I disagree; it's number one in my book. Carrot cake was one of the first cakes I baked; it accompanied me to one of my *Bake Off* auditions; it was the

first birthday cake I baked for someone – my grandma, Sheila; it was the most revered of my bakes sold at a charity bake sale and it reminds me of Saturday afternoons spent wandering around the shops with Mum when I was younger, always featuring a pit stop for a chunk of carrot cake from the café.

Carrot cake can also be adapted very easily to grace any manner of occasion: birthday cake, Easter cake, Christmas cake, wedding cake, afternoon tea – you name it, it's welcome. I therefore believe that everyone should have a carrot cake recipe up their sleeve. This bake is simple to prepare and is full of spice, sweet pecans and orange – the game-changer! Even those who are averse to carrot cake will be converted by this recipe (I have proof of this) and you will successfully send ripples of happiness out to all of the people who get to enjoy it. Now go and make this epic cake and sprinkle some fairy dust on the world.

Zest and Spice Carrot and Pecan Cake

....

Serves: approximately 12

Hands on time: 35 minutes

Cooking time: 50 minutes

....

INGREDIENTS

Cake

100g (3½oz) sultanas

Zest and juice of 2 oranges

300ml (½ pint) vegetable oil, plus extra for greasing

4 large eggs

170g (6oz) plain wholemeal flour

170g (6oz) self-raising flour

4 teaspoons ground cinnamon

4 teaspoons mixed spice

2 teaspoons bicarbonate of soda

1½ teaspoons baking powder

280g (9½oz) light brown sugar

280g (9½oz) grated carrot

100g (3½oz) pecan nuts, finely chopped

Cream Cheese Frosting

70g (2¾oz) unsalted butter, at room temperature

115g (3¾oz) cream cheese, at room temperature

350g (11½oz) icing sugar

10ml (1 dessertspoon) freshly squeezed lemon juice

Zest of 1 lemon

Candied Maple Pecans

7g (¼oz) coconut oil or unsalted butter

40g (1½oz) maple syrup

¼ teaspoon ground cinnamon

Pinch of salt

100g (3½oz) pecan nuts

To Decorate

Rosemary sprigs (optional)

METHOD

Preheat the oven to 180°C (160°C fan/350°F/Gas
Mark 4). Grease and line 2 x 20cm (8in) round tins with
baking parchment.

In a small microwavable bowl, mix the sultanas
and the zest and juice of the oranges and pop in the
microwave to warm for 1 minute.

Pour the vegetable oil into a large jug, add the eggs
and whisk with a small hand whisk to fully combine. Into a
large mixing bowl, sift the two flours, cinnamon, mixed
spice, bicarbonate of soda and baking powder before
adding the light brown sugar and mixing well to combine.
Next add the sultana mixture, grated carrot, chopped
pecans and egg mixture to the dry ingredients and mix
thoroughly with a spatula.

Pour the batter into the 2 prepared tins and bake in
the preheated oven for approximately 35 minutes, or until
a skewer inserted into the centre of the cakes comes out
clean and they are shrinking away from the sides of the
tin. Remove from the oven and leave for 5 minutes in the
tins before turning out onto a wire rack to cool.

For the cream cheese frosting, beat the butter on
high speed for a couple of minutes until slightly whipped.
Add the cream cheese in 2 stages, beating well between
each addition. Finally, add the icing sugar in 3 stages –
initially the mixture will become loose and quite sloppy;

don't panic, as you beat in the final addition of icing sugar, it will start to stiffen. If it is still very loose, you can make it stiffer by adding a little more icing sugar. Once all of the icing sugar is incorporated, add the lemon zest and juice before beating a final time to combine. Cover and set aside until ready to use.

For the candied pecans, preheat the oven to 190°C (170°C fan/375°F/Gas Mark 5) and line a baking tray with baking parchment. Put the coconut oil, maple syrup, cinnamon and salt into a small saucepan, place over a low heat and gently stir until the coconut oil has melted. Once melted, remove from the heat and add the pecans. Stir to thoroughly coat them in the sticky liquid, pour onto the prepared baking tray, spread out evenly and roast in the preheated oven for 10 minutes. Remove from the oven, gently stir around with a spatula to ensure the syrup mixture is evenly coating the nuts, then return to the oven for a final 5 minutes, before removing and allowing to cool on the tray. The nuts will begin to harden and develop a wonderful crunch as well as a fabulously fragrant, toasted flavour. Once hardened, reserve around 12 pecan halves to decorate and finely chop the remainder.

Once the cakes have completely cooled, assemble the final cake. Transfer one cake to a cake board, stand or plate. Neatly spread just under half of the cream cheese frosting over the top; use a stepped palette knife to create an even layer. Place the second cake on top, inverting it so that the bottom is on the top, to give the final cake neater edges and a flatter finish. Liberally cover the top of the cake with the remaining frosting, smoothing to finish. (You might find there is a little too much, in which case freeze it for use at a later date.) Create a pattern on top if you're feeling snazzy. Scatter the chopped candied pecans around the outside circumference of the top of the cake, then place the 12 candied pecan halves at intervals inside the circumference of the pecan crumb border. Garnish with a few rosemary sprigs for some added flourish if you wish. Slice and serve.

ᴄVariation
Switch up some of the carrot for a little grated beetroot or parsnip.

The Social Bake

Communal eating, with family, friends, even strangers is universal. For many centuries and across various cultures, food has connected and nurtured us. Nowadays, we relish opportunities to go out with friends and have a natter over cake and a coffee; dining out at a restaurant, enjoying quality food and sharing a moment with friends excites us and a Sunday roast cooked by mum, dad or the grandparents is tradition, without it the week isn't complete.

A recent study at Oxford university analysed the functions of social eating.[1] It found that eating socially resulted in people feeling happier and more satisfied with life; meanwhile, they were more trusting of others and had more friends who they could rely on for support. Not only that, the study suggested that social eating may have evolved as a mechanism for aiding social bonding.

This research doesn't come as a surprise to me. As someone who is prone to feelings of low mood and having struggled with an eating disorder, there have been episodes in my life when eating socially has been both an effort and a challenge. I have thus avoided social gatherings or dreaded experiences; at a time when things were particularly bad, my friendship circle was massively constricted. It becomes a vicious cycle of feeling low, not socializing, and thereby not experiencing the joy that accompanies social eating. Nowadays, I look forward to opportunities to enjoy food with family and friends; we laugh, make memories and savour the edible delights on offer. Ultimately, I have built stronger relationships as a result of feeling able to engage socially over food.

Besides a heightened sense of wellbeing, calm, confidence and focus, baking represents a form of altruism as well as a simple means for social interaction. Firstly, baking for others can give us meaning in life: we are providing pleasure for others and making them happy; whether it's constructing a birthday cake for a friend or making grandma her favourite tea loaf, we're sharing food with those who will appreciate it. Similarly, baking represents a fairly 'simple' medium for us to engage with people; it's on our terms and can  include as much or as little social interaction as we feel capable of on any particular day. Over time, this can help improve our social skills, build connections and thereby ignite stronger relationships.

For me, a bulletproof brownie represents the archetypal 'social bake'. Everybody likes brownie, right? Deliver a winning brownie and it's certain to please any audience. Having said this, I have a confession to make…brownie has been a baking nemesis for me since day one…why? Because I struggled to achieve my version of perfect. Over the years, I tirelessly scoured the internet for answers as to why my attempts at brownie just weren't living up to my expectations. That was until I introduced myself to Becca, a little baking wizard who I stumbled across on Instagram. Having nattered away about our mutual love of baking, she then imparted some of her incredible brownie wisdom, such that I now believe I have nailed a rich, fudgy brownie recipe which, if you follow the rules, will never fail to deliver. Not only that, through a mutual love of food, I now consider Becca my baking buddy – further proof that baking is such a wonderful means of social interaction and happiness.

Now get your bake on and whip up this filthy slab of gold; share it with a friend or two and experience an additional sense of pure joy.

Bulletproof Chocolate Fudge Brownie

....

Serves: 16   **Hands on time: 25 minutes**
                                  Cooking time: 25–30 minutes

....

INGREDIENTS

165g (5¾oz) unsalted
   butter, plus extra for
   greasing
225g (7½oz) good-quality
   dark chocolate
115g (3¾oz) golden
   caster sugar
160g (5½oz) soft light
   brown sugar

110g (3¾oz) plain flour
35g (1¼oz) good-quality
   cocoa powder
½ teaspoon fine salt
50g (2oz) milk chocolate
50g (2oz) white chocolate
3 large eggs

METHOD

Preheat the oven to 180°C (160°C fan/350°F/Gas Mark
4). Then, grease and line a 20cm (8in) square tin with
baking parchment.

Melt the butter and dark chocolate in a bowl placed
over a saucepan filled with around 2.5cm (1in) of
simmering water, stirring occasionally. Once melted, add
both the sugars to the bowl (still over the heat) and gently
stir to combine. Keep over the heat for around 5–10
minutes, allowing the sugar to dissolve a little, before
setting aside to cool for around 10 minutes.

Meanwhile, prepare the remaining ingredients: sift the flour, cocoa powder and salt into a large bowl and set aside. Chop the milk and white chocolate into small chunks. Crack the eggs into a small bowl and lightly whisk.

Once the chocolate mixture has cooled slightly, stir in the whisked eggs a little at a time – work quite quickly with each addition to prevent the eggs from scrambling. The mixture may look a little split; just continue to stir past this stage until well combined and resembling ganache in consistency.

Finally, very gently fold through the flour mixture; you want to work the mixture as little as possible. Just before you have finished folding in the dry ingredients, add the chopped chocolate and continue to fold through. Once everything is just combined, stop mixing and pour into your prepared tin. Level with a spatula and bake in the preheated oven for 25–30 minutes. When cooked it should be firm to the touch but remain soft in the centre (see Recipe tips, page 184) – the key to a decent brownie is definitely to under- rather than overbake.

Remove from the oven and leave to cool in the tin, placed on a wire rack. Once cool, transfer to the fridge for around 1 hour to set a little firmer. When you can't wait any longer, remove from the fridge and, using a very sharp knife, cut into squares – size is up to you, I suggest 16 squares. Bear in mind, this devilish beauty is blooming rich so a little goes a long way but you're the judge of how much you want/need so I'll leave that decision in your capable hands.

Variations

This is a template for a world of brownie adventure; wonderful additions include:

- Raspberries or cherries. You can use frozen raspberries, or you can dollop a few teaspoons of the sticky raspberry sauce from the Raspberry Chocolate Layer Cake (see pages 90–3) over the batter in the tin before baking.

- Similarly, you could use the salted caramel from the millionaire's shortbread on pages 124–7 and dollop it across the top of the batter before baking for a wicked salted caramel brownie.

- Stir through toasted nuts – Brazil nuts, pistachios and pecans work wonderfully I find.

Recipe tips

- Where possible use good-quality ingredients; 70% dark chocolate is my preference, butter with a high fat ratio (above 80%), and good-quality cocoa powder.

- Inserting a skewer into a brownie isn't a great method of testing its readiness. My best advice here is: it shouldn't wobble in the middle of the brownie if you give the tray a little shake. If it does, pop it back in the oven for 5 more minutes. If you touch the top it should feel firm enough that you don't punch through the skin with very little force. Underneath, it will still be gooey – it sets firmer as it cools but remains wonderfully truffle-y and rich.

The Meaning Behind a Bake

Since my interest in baking has grown, so too have my understanding and appreciation of food. It's only when you spend a little longer thinking about and researching the topic that you appreciate just how much value we attach to food. Across different cultures, in countries around the world, through generations, and in religious communities, foods are used to symbolize aspects of faith, commemorate festivals or heroes and mark special dates or seasons. I think that each and every one of us attaches meaning to certain foods, from mince pies at Christmas and simnel cake at Easter to pancakes for Shrove Tuesday and even half-time orange slices during sports matches; food is symbolic and heart-warming.

There is something about these sentimental bakes that makes them all the more enjoyable, both to prepare and consume. The other common theme is that they are generally enjoyed with others, which again exemplifies the importance of human connection. When we come together to celebrate a moment in time, homemade food is at the heart of the occasion. The happiness experienced by everyone is palpable, the moment is marked and memories are made.

Our foodie traditions aren't necessarily led by others or history, they can be extremely personal too. I remember with fondness lapping up jam sandwiches as fuel before a race when I competed; to this day, I still consider them one of the best energy-packed snacks (homemade strawberry jam on homemade bread really takes this concept up a notch). Meanwhile, jam doughnuts are a go-to for Mum and I following a particularly demanding task or challenge. I don't consider food a reward in this instance, but an acknowledgement of the moment, a physical 'need' and the ultimate satisfaction. What I also love is that time doesn't limit us in terms of the rise of new rituals; they are unique and become woven into our lives through shared experiences.

Preparing bakes that have personal or historical meaning can help us detach from the 'self'; channelling our energy into a constructive endeavour, one that carries meaning. When we really begin to doubt our abilities or worth, we can fall into a deep sea of negativity and self-pity. Learning and understanding the significance of a bake and its connotation for others, or simply remembering a personal experience, can leave us inspired. Inspiration then drives us forward; whether its transient or more enduring, we start to feel good about our direction and purpose. Not only that, bakes of this kind allow us to remember moments in our past, rediscover joy and share our creativity with others.

I'm a huge sport fan, I live for spring and summer, hibernating in winter, and I've always loved fruit. In fact, I find myself trying to squeeze some fruit (or veg) into almost all of my recipes. It's unsurprising, then, this recipe combines the three. Think Wimbledon and the tradition of strawberries and cream – a time I eagerly anticipate each year – paired with an ultimate of summer desserts, cheesecake. Each element of this recipe gives me a sense of happiness. I've taken to preparing it in July to mark the start of Wimbledon, but really, I'm not limited by this. I bring it out on occasions throughout the year – it turns out most people are partial to a slice of cheesecake. It extracts me from moments of doom and it's a much-needed ray of sunshine on the cloudiest of days.

Your version of foodie traditions may look very different to mine and, thus, I encourage you to embrace your own memories and preferences; cheesecakes are, however, a perfect vehicle for channelling any manner of flavour combinations, and honestly, this strawberries and cream combo is wildly good.

Strawberries and Cream Cheesecake

Serves: 16

Hands on time: 40 minutes
Setting time: 9 hours

INGREDIENTS

Buttery Biscuit Base
100g (3½oz) unsalted
    butter, plus extra for
    greasing
200g (7oz) digestive
    biscuits

Cheesecake
210g (7¼oz) double cream
450g (14½oz) cream cheese
70g (2¾oz) icing sugar
¼ teaspoon vanilla bean
    paste
2 teaspoons freshly
    squeezed lemon juice

Strawberry Sauce
400g (13oz) strawberries
110g (3¾oz) caster sugar
Squeeze of lemon juice

To Decorate
Handful of strawberries
Approximately 5 mint
    leaves

METHOD
Grease the sides of a 20cm (8in) round spring form tin, and line the bottom with 20cm (8in) cake board.

Place the butter in a heatproof bowl and melt in the microwave or place in a small saucepan over a low heat.

Crush the biscuits by placing in a sealable freezer bag and use a rolling bin to bash the biscuits to form a fairly uniform fine crumb, then transfer to a large bowl.

Pour the melted butter over the crushed biscuits and mix thoroughly. Tip the buttery biscuit mixture into the prepared tin and press down firmly to form an even layer. Transfer to the fridge and allow to set for at least 1 hour – longer is fine.

Prepare the strawberry sauce. Hull and quarter the strawberries and transfer to a large saucepan. Add the sugar and lemon juice. Place over a low–medium heat and stir to ensure the sugar is well distributed before bringing to a gentle simmer. Reduce the heat and allow to bubble gently for around 15 minutes. Stir occasionally to ensure it isn't catching and as the fruit starts to soften, crush it with a fork or masher.

Once the sauce has visibly thickened – don't worry if yours takes longer than 15 minutes – remove from the heat and while still warm, pass through a sieve, using the back of a spoon to push through. This can take a little time but get as much of the juice out of the mixture as you can. You should end up with a minimum of 160g–200g (5½–7oz) of sauce once it has been sieved. If you're worried that the sauce is too thin, you can pop it back over the heat in a clean saucepan and reduce a little more. Set aside to cool fully before using – it should thicken up further!

Once the base has set firm, prepare the filling. Pour the double cream into a medium bowl and whisk using an electric whisk or stand mixer until it forms medium to stiff peaks; this will take 4–5 minutes. Combine the cream cheese, icing sugar, vanilla and lemon juice in a separate large bowl. Whisk for 2–3 minutes until the ingredients are well combined and the mixture is smooth. Add the whipped cream to the cream cheese mixture and briefly whisk a final time for around 30 seconds, ensuring that the mixture is nice and thick and holds its shape.

Remove the biscuit base from the fridge. Spoon over approximately one-third of the cheesecake mixture, levelling with a palette knife. Using a teaspoon, dot blobs around 50g (2oz) each of the strawberry sauce evenly across the top of the cream cheese layer. Use a toothpick to delicately drag the blobs of sauce to create a ripple effect – don't agitate the mixture too much or it will blend.

Next, carefully dollop another third of the cheesecake mixture over the strawberry ripple in approximately four spoonfuls – top, bottom, left and right. Using a palette knife or the back of a spoon, very gently drag the cream cheese evenly over the ripple taking care not to blend the ripple beneath too much – this doesn't need to be too neat.

Repeat with another layer of strawberry sauce ripple before topping with the remaining cheesecake mixture. Level the top of the cheesecake off as neatly as you can before transferring to the fridge for a minimum of 8 hours, and preferably overnight.

When you are ready to serve, run a sharp knife carefully around the outside edge of the cheesecake; alternatively warm a tea towel over a radiator and hold it against the sides of the tin for 20–30 seconds. Carefully release the catch on the tin and lift it off.

Neaten the edges of the cheesecake by smoothing with a palette knife. Drizzle or pipe the remainder of the strawberry sauce across the top of the cheesecake in a haphazard fashion. Slice a handful of strawberries and scatter in the centre along with a few sprigs of mint leaves, to decorate.

*Serve with a glass of fizz...*and more strawberries and maybe more cream because...why NOT? Enjoy!

Recipe tips

- Cheesecake left over? Cover tightly and freeze for up to 2 months, thawing overnight in the fridge before serving.

- This is a good dessert to prepare the day before you wish to serve – less stress and fuss on the day.

Baking
with
Others

I've got to admit that, while I enjoy baking with others in mind, I don't generally bake with others. I guess I quite selfishly take all of the pleasure from the experience for myself. I like to be in control in the kitchen, to see a process through from beginning to end, to be responsible at every stage and to stand back and admire my work on completion.

As with many things though, a process enjoyed with others can elicit huge joy; the experience may be quite different but the happiness is unavoidable. For those who face mental-health struggles, there is often a risk of becoming socially withdrawn, isolating from people and avoiding group activities. I know I have been a victim of this in the past, and while I don't believe we should condemn ourselves for any behaviours or feelings, it's helpful to be able to acknowledge that it's far from favourable to fall into this trap. By challenging ourselves to face the uncomfortable, we can silence some of the negative emotions. Low-pressure situations can feel less scary, and actually the company of another person can make us feel safer and less vulnerable if something goes 'wrong'.

Engaging in a hobby with like-minded people can also help us foster friendships with others, expand our knowledge and occupy us in a positive way, even imposing routine in the form of a weekly class or arranged group exploit. Baking with family, especially children, can also be fantastic. Modelling behaviour to children can really help to teach them new skills while strengthening adult–child bonds. Meanwhile, sharing the fun of baking with friends creates richer experiences, ones when happy moments become magical memories.

Now, it's entirely acceptable to bake a masterpiece with a friend or to call on someone's help when you are facing a mighty baking challenge, one that would be aided by some moral support. However, when the priority is more the sociability of the activity, I find that the bake needs to

be fairly straightforward. A finger-licking classic that is open to a bit of creativity is what is required, I think. Of course, there are any manner of things you can try your hand at but, for me, the winner is a fridge cake. Tiffin, rocky road, refrigerator cake; call it what you want, it's my go-to social bake.

Fridge cake is entirely adaptable to the audience; from the mysterious and sophisticated dark-chocolate eaters to those who enjoy the sickly sweetness of white chocolate, we can accommodate anyone. Better than that, it's great for using up old ingredients, or odds and ends that are left lurking in the cupboards or hanging around after Christmas and Easter – I think of it as a trash bake as it makes use of stuff that might otherwise end up in the bin.

I get too excited when it comes to this humble snack. IT'S JUST SO GOOD. The recipe I have provided is full of milky smoothness; it's sweet, buttery and has hints of caramel from the Biscoff biscuits. Obviously, I think it's imperative that you give this recipe a try but don't be limited by these ingredients – incorporate your favourite flavours, chocolate varieties and opt for alternative extras. Together with your friend or family member plan something that meets everyone's requirements and then get to work!

The 'Everything You Could Wish For' Fridge Cake

Makes: 16 generous pieces

Hands on time: 15 minutes

**Cooking time: 5 minutes +
2 hours setting time**

INGREDIENTS

Base

165g (5¾oz) unsalted
butter, plus extra for
greasing
50g (2oz) caster sugar
65g (2½oz) golden syrup
25g (1oz) cocoa powder
245g (7¾oz) Biscoff biscuits
Pinch of salt

55g (2oz) mixed roasted
(even salted) nuts,
roughly chopped (see
Recipe tips)

Topping

140g (5oz) milk chocolate
110g (3¾oz) dark chocolate

55g (2oz) dried fruit, such
as sultanas, raisins,
cherries, cranberries
10–15 chocolates from a
miniature chocolate
selection box

195

METHOD

Grease and line a 20cm (8in) square cake tin with baking parchment.

Put the butter, caster sugar, golden syrup and cocoa powder in a medium saucepan placed over a low heat. Stir periodically until melted then set aside.

Put the biscuits in a freezer bag and crush with a rolling pin. Then place in a large bowl with a pinch of salt. Add the nuts and dried fruit.

Pour the liquid mixture over the dry ingredients and stir well to evenly coat. Next chop up the miniature chocolates into small chunks. Add to the bowl and stir to distribute – don't overmix at this point as the residual heat from the liquid will start to melt the chocolates. Tip into the prepared tin and press down firmly with a spatula or the back of a spoon. Pop into the fridge while you prepare the chocolate topping.

Put the milk and dark chocolate into a medium-sized bowl and place over a pan of gently simmering water. Gently heat the chocolate mixture until fully melted, stirring occasionally.

Recipe tips

- It's worth noting that the more additions you make
  to the base of these things, the more fragile they
  can become when slicing. Ultimately, they will
  always taste great but if you are striving for neatness
  it can become an issue if there is too much in the
  way of extras.

- Along a similar line, make sure that
  biscuits aren't left too chunky –
  obviously they shouldn't be crushed
  to oblivion either; small nuggets
  are perfect. Also, chop large
  nuts in halves or into quarters.

Remove the base from the fridge and evenly drizzle
the liquid chocolate over the top, then pick up the tin and
gently rock from side to side, encouraging the chocolate
to evenly coat the base and create a smooth layer.
Alternatively, you can use a stepped palette knife to level.
Return to the fridge for 2 hours to set.

To cut the fridge cake, run a sharp knife under warm
water, carefully wipe dry, then cut into 16 even squares.

The Pure Unadulterated JOY of Baking... and Eating

I'm not sure there is anything as universally agreeable as a chocolate chip cookie...that's a pretty bold statement I know, but I'm quite confident in my conviction here.

The humble chocolate chip cookie has cemented itself as a staple in our homes, at bake sales and in bakeries. Chocolate chip cookie dough has even managed to muscle its way into ice cream, really stamping its authority over our lives. Apparently created by accident in the 1930s, they have now become a feature in almost every baker's cookbook. Surely it's safe to say that the sweet joy of a chocolate chip cookie is unanimously agreed?

As mentioned on a number of occasions already, nostalgia is particularly powerful when it comes to food and cookies are no exception. I believe that, if encouraged, so many of us could look back on moments in our past that included a chocolate chip cookie – best served warm alongside a cold

glass of fresh milk, after a gruelling playtime outside. OK, maybe that's just me! Regardless, what's incredible is that past enjoyment, occasions and happiness can be vividly recalled when we chomp down on countless cookies across our lifetime, and the satisfaction experienced with each subsequent chocolate chip cookie encounter is intensified by our previous experiences.

As it happens, there is some chemical-y science that backs this up too. The ratio of sugar and fat in a chocolate cookie seems to represent perfection when it comes to desirability and satisfaction. Scientists have found that this 'cocktail' of ingredients is capable of activating the same reward circuits in the brain that are triggered by addictive drugs and alcohol. The brain's response to these foods is a release of dopamine which gives us an intense feeling of pleasure. Similarly, as mentioned on page 152, chocolate itself contains small amounts of compounds that target the receptors in the brain responsible for releasing mood-enhancing chemicals; when combined with sugar the feelings of pleasure are intensified. This isn't to say that chocolate chip cookies are akin to drugs, nor is it a reason to consider them an 'addictive' food choice. In fact, we need no justification for our enjoyment of a chocolate chip cookie. In my opinion, it's just more reason to embrace our much-loved favourite for all its mood-enhancing benefits.

Since their invention, people have been in pursuit of the ultimate chocolate chip cookie. Some relatively extensive research has led me to the belief, however, that a few things take this bake from really good to sublime. Quality ingredients are a good place to start, some really great butter with a fat content of 80 per cent+ is a winner; the blend of sugars creates a balance of chew and crisp; some quality chocolate is a must; roasting the nuts adds depth of flavour; salt intensifies the sweetness; meanwhile vanilla contrasts with the chocolate chips, resulting in a well-rounded bake.

Besides the satisfaction that accompanies the eating, the mood boost and the nostalgia locked up in a chocolate chip cookie, there is of course the reward involved in producing these beauties. And really, it draws on just about everything we have discussed so far. The meditative practice, with various elements, a degree of focus to execute each stage, some creativity if you fancy, inevitable mistakes – the confidence boost when you create some bakery-worthy delights, shared with friends or made with the kids. This bake is happiness through and through.

Next-level Chocolate Chip Cookies

Serves 14

Hands on time: 20 minutes plus 2–48 hours resting time
Cooking Time: 17 minutes (up to 34 minutes if you need to bake in 2 batches)

INGREDIENTS

115g (3¾oz) softened unsalted butter
120g (3¾oz) light brown sugar
100g (3½oz) caster sugar
1 large egg, lightly beaten
½ teaspoon vanilla extract
250g (8oz) plain flour
½ teaspoon bicarbonate of soda
½ teaspoon baking powder
½ teaspoon salt
60g (2½oz) Daim chocolate (2 average-sized Daim bars), broken into small chunks

50g (2oz) good-quality milk chocolate (approximately 50– 60% cocoa solids), chopped into small chunks, or Callets™ (see Recipe tips, page 203)
50g (2oz) good-quality white chocolate, chopped into small chunks, or Callets™ (see Recipe tips, page 203)
40g (1½oz) roasted salted macadamia nuts

METHOD

First prepare the cookie dough. In a large mixing bowl, beat the butter and both sugars until pale and slightly fluffy. Add the lightly beaten egg a little at a time, beating well between each addition, followed by the vanilla.

Gently stir in the flour, bicarbonate of soda, baking powder and salt, until the mixture just comes together. Gradually fold through the Daim, milk and white chocolate chunks and macadamia nuts. If using a stand mixer, use a low setting and mix until the ingredients are just combined. Cover and refrigerate for anywhere between 2 and 48 hours – I know this sounds like forEVER, but somehow it really helps to enhance the toasted caramel flavour we know and love in a cookie. If you just can't wait that long, a couple of hours will be fine, but next time, please try the extra resting time and experience the full glory.

Once the dough has rested, preheat the oven to 180°C (160°C fan/350°F/Gas Mark 4) and line 2 large baking sheets with baking parchment.

Remove the cookie dough from the fridge and roll into approximately 14 x 60g (2½oz) balls. Distribute these on the baking sheets, allowing plenty of space between them, and bake in the preheated oven for around 17 minutes or until golden round the edges but still soft in the middle. After 10 minutes, remove one tray from the oven and give it a firm bang on the work surface, return it to the oven and repeat with the other baking tray. Repeat this process again at around 13 minutes. The tray-banging process isn't essential but creates ripples across the surface of the cookies which gives great texture.

Once baked, remove the trays from the oven, perform one bang of each tray on the work surface then leave the cookies to cool for 5 minutes on the baking tray before transferring to a wire rack to cool completely.

Recipe tips

- Callets™ are large chocolate chips formulated for baking. They are available at specialist baking stockists and online.

- If you need to bake in batches, keep the reserved balls of cookie dough in the fridge while your first batch bakes and cook the next batch immediately.

- You can freeze the raw cookie dough balls. When in need, remove one from the freezer and either thaw overnight in the fridge or for a couple of hours at room temperature and bake as above or bake from frozen for an 'anytime' cookie hit. The cooking time will be an extra 3–5 minutes (keep an eye on the colour) and don't start the tray banging until around 13–15 minutes.

End Notes

CHAPTER 2

1 https://www.huffingtonpost.co.uk/entry/baking-for-others-psychology_n_58dd0b85e4b0e6ac7092aaf8

2 Kim, J-H., Choe, K., Lee, K., 'Effects of food art therapy on the self-esteem, self-expression, and social skills of persons with mental illness in community rehabilitation facilities', *Healthcare* 2020, 8, 428

3 https://www.escoffieronline.com/how-baking-for-others-can-improve-your-mental-health/

CHAPTER 3

1 Haley, L. & McKay, E., '"Baking gives you confidence": users' views of engaging in the occupation of baking', *The British Journal of Occupational Therapy*, (2004)

2 https://www.apa.org/pubs/journals/releases/bul-bul0000138.pdf

CHAPTER 4

1 https://www.nursingtimes.net/archive/cookery-lessons-aid-recovery-from-eating-disorders-18-12-2009/

2 https://www.ninds.nih.gov/Disorders/Patient-Caregiver-Education/Understanding-Sleep

3 Zizza C.A., 'Healthy snacking recommendations: one size does not fit all', https://pubmed.ncbi.nlm.nih.gov/24518869/

4 Martin C.R., et al., 'The brain-gut-microbiome axis', https://www.ncbi.nlm.nih.gov/pmc/articles/PMC6047317/

Mayer E.A., et al., 'Gut microbes and the brain: paradigm shift in neuroscience', https://www.ncbi.nlm.nih.gov/pmc/articles/PMC4228144/

5 Martin P., 'The epidemiology of anxiety disorders: a review', https://pubmed.ncbi.nlm.nih.gov/22034470/

Gosling J.A., et al., 'Online insomnia treatment and the reduction of anxiety symptoms as a secondary outcome in a randomised controlled trial: The role of cognitive-behavioural factors', https://pubmed.ncbi.nlm.nih.gov/29717621/

CHAPTER 5

1 Dunbar, R.I.M., 'Breaking bread: the functions of social eating', *Adaptive Human Behavior and Physiology* (2017), https://doi.org/10.1007/s40750-017-0061-4

Index

A Note on Ovens

Oven temperatures can vary hugely – they often run too hot or too cool, bake unevenly or are altogether inconsistent. My best advice for this is firstly to invest in an oven thermometer – you can move it around your oven to test if there are hot spots, and generally learn a little more about how your oven works. Secondly, it's really a case of trial and error. For the best results in your kitchen, you need to learn the characteristics of the equipment you are working with. Take notes each time you bake, then tweak and amend until perfect – you've got this!

Acknowledgements

A heartfelt thank you to Philippa Wilkinson and Julia Shone for your unconditional support; without your belief in me, I could not have completed this book. I consider you both friends for life. My gratitude also extends to the whole team at Greenfinch for bringing this book to life – I still can't quite believe it is a reality.

A special thank you to my family, for your love and support throughout, and friends; chief recipe testers; Liz, Bill, Claire & Simon; Sally for putting up with my endless worry and physio Mark for doubling up as a counsellor – I feel forever in debt to you. Finally a massive thank you to Mum; without your love, support and wisdom, none of this would have been possible. Love you.